Faith

Wave

Faith *Wave*

I think...
therefore
it is

Peter Baksa

Faith Wave by Peter Baksa

©2012. Intelegance Publishing, LLC, Chicago, Illinois

Fulfillment, warehousing and distribution contact books@peterbaksa.com
AtlasBooks
30 Amberwood Parkway
Ashland, OH 44805

Contact: books@peterbaksa.com

Inquiries: Contact books@peterbaksa.com with requests for quantity
                discounts or orders for educational institutions.

Orders: You may also order directly from Peterbaksa.com or
                Amazon.com

Design by Indigo Design, Inc.
www.bookcoverdesignbyindigo.com

Library of Congress Control Number: 2012939020
ISBN 978-0-9832472-6-5

Printed in the United States of America

CONTENTS

INTRODUCTION
  Reality as a Manifestation of Our Thoughts 1

PART ONE

THE SCIENCE

CHAPTER 1
  Quantum Mechanics Basics 7

CHAPTER 2
  The Uncertainty Principle and Entanglement 15

CHAPTER 3
  The Mind and Quantum Mechanics 23

CHAPTER 4
  Brain Waves 31

CHAPTER 5
  Neuroplasticity 39

CHAPTER 6
  The Zero Point Field 49

CHAPTER 7
The ZPF and Mass 61

PART TWO

THE SPIRITUAL

CHAPTER 8
Religions of Abraham **69**

CHAPTER 9
Religions of Insight **77**

CHAPTER 10
Miracles **87**

CHAPTER 11
Meditation, Prayer, and Faith **97**

CHAPTER 12
Meditating on Miracles **107**

CHAPTER 13
Magic **115**

PART THREE

THE EXPLANATION

CHAPTER 14
Science versus Religion **125**

CHAPTER 15
What Is God **135**

CHAPTER 16
Belief versus Imagining **143**

CHAPTER 17
Tibetan Monks..**149**

CHAPTER 18
Healing and Faith...**157**

CHAPTER 19
Altered States of Consciousness.................**167**

CHAPTER 20
Conclusions...**175**

Notes...**179**

"The path to manifesting the life of your dreams."

"Peter Baksa, with remarkable clarity, fuses the insights of modern physics with those of traditional religion. He rejects the mechanistic materialism that still dominates the western mind, seeing the physical world as a manifestation of spiritual energy. Anyone interested in making sense of either physics or religion – or both – will gain great inspiration from this book."

—Robert Van de Weyer, Anglican minister in Cambridgeshire, England; lecturer for twenty five years in Cambridge on economics, philosophy and religion; and author of over 50 books

"What has quantum physics have to do with prayer and meditation? Or, how could the world's different religion's hold similarities to one another? Author Peter Baksa weaves seemingly unrelated fields of study into a convergence: *Faith Wave*."

—The Rev. Dr. Glenda W Prins, author of Lessons from Katherine: A Spiritual Struggle.

"Peter Baksa explains there is no conflict between modern science and ancient religions. With this understanding, the author empowers the reader to practice the powers latent in the human mind. Ancient approaches to healing body, mind, and spirit are embedded in the world's religions such as diet and exercise, healing by touch, human energy field, pray and meditate."

— Michael Turk, a nationally known practitioner, teacher, and author on the use of acupuncture, massage, and moxibustion to treat chronic pain and disability

"Finally, a book that correlates quantum science with religious affections. Peter Baksa calls it *Faith Wave*; brain circuits of positive emotions. Peter's work does for prayer and meditation what my work does for spirituality and creative acts of transformation."

—*Dr. Carolyn Reinhart, author of We Are One*

"With my focus on good mental health, I am pleased with the holistic approach Peter Baksa takes in this book, especially how we can strengthen our minds and bodies as transmitters of Faith Wave."

—*Elaine Campbell, M.D., author of My Life as a Car: A Mental Wellness Guide in Your Glove Compartment*

Introduction

REALITY
AS A MANIFESTATION
OF OUR THOUGHTS

Thoughts affect our reality, manifest in it, and direct it. Matter is made up of energy, and thought is a form of energy. Therefore, our reality is a manifestation of our thoughts. We will investigate how this happens, and more importantly how we train our brain to create what I term *Faith Wave*. This wave enhances our ability to engage with what some call God to initiate the manifestation process. For millennia and around the world, some religions have advocated the power of prayer; other religions, the power of meditation. Pray and you will get what you desire, what you need; ask and it shall be given.

Yet, in our modern world, such assertions can be dismissed as unscientific or religious superstition. We are encouraged to work harder and, if needed at all, save any prayers for Sunday church. This is what I once thought. Yet, what if those ancient religions really have a point? What if all theology was doing was simplifying the truths so that the masses might understand?

Or, turn this situation around. How would you explain to someone from four thousand years ago how stars form, evolution sponsors ever-new adaptations, or quantum mechanics explains the connection all reality? Well, you wouldn't; they'd never understand. You would simply give an analogy or tell them a parable they *would* understand, and then encourage them to have faith that what you told them was the truth.

Now through science, we are just beginning to delve into what theology has been trying to make us understand. We know about quantum mechanics and entanglement, and we know that energy and matter refer to the same concept. Hence, it is a simple enough concept for us now, yet impossible for anyone to have grasped a few thousand years ago.

Prayer, or any form of meditation for that matter, is a focus of directed brain waves entering the Zero Point Field.[1] These entangled waves are sending back exactly what we send out. My research of ancient theological texts and interviews that I conducted while living among Tibetan Monks in Beijing China all seemed to point to the idea that there was something we as humans can do better to communicate with "god" (universal laws and principles that create everything).[2]

One of the common denominators that I found in every religious text was the idea of quieting the mind and directing or focusing on a specific thought or intention. Some called this prayer, some called this mediation, and some had similar titles for this same activity, but it all concluded the same idea of a quiet mind. When we quiet the mind and focus on a thought, we teach our brain to go into a state, which results in a specific type brain wave. My first book, *The Point of Power*, goes into a great deal of theoretical detail, but it points in the direction that our thoughts are at the essence of what creates our life situations. In this book we posit that the mind can be trained to go into a specific waveform that allows us to initiate an intention more efficiently.[3]

This wave (*Faith Wave*) allows us to connect to everything and communicate by initiating a transaction at the quantum level, which causes the law of attraction to activate and become directed. In order to achieve what I call *Faith Wave*, we must train our brain. The monks that I interviewed at the Lama Temple seemed to start each day with a ritual of "feeding the Buddha." This is a similar ritual to the Catholic mass, which involves drinking the blood and eating the flesh of Christ. I perceive the practice of these rituals to be primitive especially considering that we now live in a modern society. It is reminiscent of praying to a statue or sacrificing a person or an animal to a make-believe god.

After spending time with the Tibetan Monks, however, it became clear to me that these were not ignorant humans practicing an ancient ritual because they did not know better. Instead, they were training their brains to refine the brainwaves they were emitting. They were transcending into a meditative state to train the brain to go into what I term as Faith Wave state so as to better communicate with "the Buddha." We are able to most efficiently manifest our desires while the brain is sending out a Faith Wave with a clear focused intention, This helps explain why some theories—like those offered in books, such as *The Secret*—do or do not work.

The brain operates at a number of frequencies, generating a series of different types of brain waves. Each brain wave has its own function, and each set of waves has its own frequency range, which is designated by a different letter of the Greek alphabet. It starts with Alpha Waves at the low end, and then climbs up through Beta, Theta, Delta, and finally Gamma:

- Alpha waves pick up while we're relaxed.
- Beta waves are for our conscious daily activities.
- Theta brain waves, measured at 4-7 Hz, are the brain state of REM sleep (dreams), hypnosis, lucid dreaming, and the barely conscious state just before sleeping and just after waking. Theta is the border between the conscious and the subconscious world, and by learning to use a conscious, waking Theta brain wave we can access and influence the powerful subconscious part of ourselves that is normally inaccessible to our waking minds.

· Delta waves occur while we're unconscious.

· Gamma waves are thought to lead to improved mental focus and higher levels of consciousness, but they have been observed working in conjunction with Alpha and Theta.[4]

So, which one are we using when in our "point of power?" The simple answer would be Gamma, although Alpha lends the necessary detachment and sense of being connected that is needed for communicating with the Zero Point Field. Beta is completely ignored during times of high Gamma activity.

What we have just defined is a state of relaxation near to unconsciousness, which is the state achieved by monks in deep meditation. In other words, we have just defined a prayer. A specific overlay of our measurable brain waves led in chief by the Gamma and heralded by Alpha and Theta. But can this Faith Wave really be measured? Quantified? Does it have any real bearing on the components of our reality? Richard Davidson of the University of Wisconsin, in his work with the Dali Lama, seems to think so.[5] The Dali Lama and other monks have been training their brains their entire lives on how to manifest their own reality via their faith in the Buddha. They have done so through such simple processes as meditation. This is something the ancients had given us long before we ever knew about quantum mechanics.

More than a few think that science and theology are incompatible extremes. Now we can begin to unveil the truth: Theology is merely the simpler version of universal truths. Prayer and the precepts of theology are merely the tip of the iceberg that quantum mechanics is beginning to uncover.[6]

As a race, we are more advanced now and better able to handle the complexities behind the simple act of folding our hands together and bowing our head. So let's take another look at this now, see how our thoughts can manifest in our reality, and then see what theology has been telling us historically on the subject. We just may find some surprising similarities.

Part One

THE SCIENCE

Chapter 1

QUANTUM MECHANICS BASICS

A boundary is fixed between science and philosophy as well as reality and fantasy. That boundary is called quantum mechanics, which is the stepping-stone between the Universe, ourselves, and what we want. Quantum mechanics explains the process of how we can actually cause manifestation to happen. Taken all together, this theory could be described as science meets the Twilight Zone. So, even if it sounds zany, for our purposes it is the most important theory. Part One describes quantum mechanics in an economy of words.[1]

Photons

It all starts with the photon, which is a little corpuscle of light. A photon is a packet of energy of a given wavelength. We know it has wavelengths because we can see light of certain wavelengths, such as, red, blue, and yellow. Infrared, ultraviolet, and Gamma rays are also wavelengths, but these cannot be seen by our eyes.

Max Planck defined an equation to describe the energy of light. He said that a given photon's energy is equal to its frequency (v) times a constant named after him (h), which is called Planck's constant. This simple formula is written as:

$$E = h\,v,$$

Planck's constant is a tiny number, equal to 6.63×10^{-34} Joule-seconds, which means this number has lots of zeros between the decimal point and the 6.63. Because it is such a small number, we can expect the energy of a single photon to likewise be minuscule. Yet remember that any given beam of light contains far more photons than there are ants in the hometown where you grew up.[2]

Albert Einstein, one of Quantum Mechanic's detractors, made an important contribution, he said that energy and matter are the same thing and that all matter is comprised of energy. His equation is the more famous:

$$E=mc^2$$

Energy (E) yielded is equal to an object's mass (m) multiplied by the speed of light squared (c^2). So all matter—you, me, this book you're reading—is made up of energy. And the amount of this energy is fairly high.

What, then, is energy? Einstein said that light is, in fact, a very small particle with the energy described by Planck's equation, so energy in it's purest form is carried by photons of light. Thus, all of us are made up of constrained light.[3]

Notice that light has been defined both as a particle with discrete packets of energy and as a wavelength. So is it particle or wave? The answer is that it's both.

We now have two of the basic precepts of quantum mechanics.

1. Energy is not a continuous stream, but actually a stream of discrete, very small, units that we call *quanta*.

2. Photons behave like both particles and waves.

These precepts sounded pretty weird at first, but as scientists thought it over, they realized that it explained why electrons are found only in certain specific energy levels.[4]

Energy makes up matter; electrons are a form of matter; so electrons are made up of energy, namely, photons. Light being comprised of streams of individual particles then forces electrons to inhabit only specific energy levels when in orbit around the nucleus of an atom. When an electron gives up or receives energy, it is doing so in the form of giving up or receiving photons of light (of which it is comprised). Because photons are seen to come in discrete packets and not continuous streams of energy, then an electron is limited to exchanging energy solely in multiples of these minimal packets of energy. No fractional amounts of a single photon are allowed. When in orbit around the nucleus of an atom then, if an electron is to move closer to or farther away from the nucleus (that is, raise or lower its energy), it can do so only in multiples of a photon's energy. An electron can obtain only specific levels of energy in orbit around the nucleus. It's like the rungs on a ladder; you can't climb up half a step. The rungs would be the energy levels and the spacing between the rungs determined by the size of a photon.

This insistence on discrete energy levels dictates how atoms interact with one another. This forms the chemistry of bulk matter—everything from us to the stars. So it can be seen that the nature of the very smallest of things can have a tremendous impact on everything else including the nature of our reality. This is the reason I believe a mere thought can change our life in the natural world.

Particle-Wave Duality

Oceans have rhythmic waves coming ashore, with smooth undulating lines and no gaps or sudden bumps. A particle is a point source, a rock on the beach of our mythical sea. Quantum mechanics says that light is both a particle and a wave. By inference, so must the matter be of which they comprise. Is matter both the rock and the sea ripple?[5]

This particle-wave duality may be difficult to grasp, but is the easiest to demonstrate. You can do it yourself in a little something called the double-slit experiment. Simply take two slits, very close together; shine a light through them from one side and have a detector ready on the other. First try it one slit at a time. The results are just as if you'd shot a bullet through a single slit: the scattering of bullet debris on the other side is greatest opposite the center of the one slit and decreases the farther away you go. But now bring in two slits. For bullets you get the sum of the individual slits, the greatest concentration of debris found in the middle of the two slits. But for light? The result is closer to if you'd used water; radiating waves that overlap, constructively and destructively interfere with one another, forming a large hump in the center then a pattern of gradually decreasing highs and lows the farther away you go. The photon is now a wave.

If you want to confirm this, then just go to your local shooting range and set up the same sort of experiment, only using a gun in place of a light beam and a sandbag as the detector. First, cover up one slit and start shooting, then the other, and finally shoot with both slits exposed. Even with both slits open, you will see a concentration in the middle that sums up to that from each slit individually, smoothly dropping off the farther away it goes.

The wave effect can be seen with a pond of water. Divide the pond in two by a cardboard or metal divider with just the slits in the middle to let the water through, then place a wave generator on one side of the divide (or alternately, just start kicking your feet in the water), and a wave detector on the other side to measure the height of the waves (or, if you've a good eye, just watch the pattern of the ripples that come through the water). You will see the gradually decreasing up and down sine waves coming through.

So, light is a wave, but we haven't seen it act as a particle yet. This is actually an easy experiment that we could even conduct ourselves. Take out a flashlight and shine it at a mirror. The beam deflects off the mirror at an angle equal to that which it hit the mirror at. It creates simple straight lines just like a bullet ricocheting off a wall. Light is now a particle.

One fundamental principle of quantum mechanics is that it can be a bullet or water and a particle or simply a wave, and from there a building block for everything from the micro—to the macro-world. Yet, as Einstein declared, matter and energy are pretty much the same thing, so if our particle of energy can behave as both, then should not also that which they are the building blocks of too behave as both? Experiments have been done with neutrons and with electrons; the results are the same. So sometimes a particle acts like a particle and other times it acts like a wave. How is this possible?

Seventy years ago a solution came in the form of the Copenhagen Interpretation. Rather than being solar systems of little round shapes, atoms are actually tiny clouds of probability. Every atomic particle is neither stable nor solid, but exists as a potential of any of its future forms. This is called the *superposition* or sum of all probabilities. In this, a particle is what you measure it to be, that it is neither particle nor wave until it has been measured. This comes from a fundamental lesson in quantum mechanics: An observation is only valid in the context of the experiment in which it is performed. The key is your initial conditions.[6]

Take this example. If you want to measure an object's length, you bring a ruler. With it you can determine the object's length, width, and height. You can determine that it has dimension, so you say that it is a three-dimensional object. But, what have you learned about its weight? You have learned absolutely nothing because you brought the wrong measuring stick. Now bring a scale. You can determine that now that it has weight, and mass, but you can determine absolutely nothing about its dimensions. If you'd thought dimension and mass were two separate things then you'd be pretty confused right now about how something could have both. We know, of course, that all objects have both dimension and mass, so it just depends on what you're setting up to measure.

Particle-wave duality is exactly like that. Just like dimension and mass are two aspects of the same object, so is a photon both like a particle and a wave. The Copenhagen Interpretation is then a "generic" interpretation that does not try to say any more than that which can be proven. The Copenhagen Interpretation not without flaw, but is still the best explanation that anyone has been able to come up with in the last 70 years.

Schrödinger Wave Equation

Around the time that Max Planck was working on quantum mechanics, Erwin Schrödinger developed his own equation to describe the motions of light and the Electro-Magnetic spectrum. His equations were in the form of differential equations (calculus), while those used to describe quantum mechanics used matrices. A mathematical comparison proved that both were equivalent. In fact, the wave equations said that waves are three dimensional, meaning that light waves can behave like particles. They even described how particles, like electrons, could jump from one energy state to another, so even described in terms of wave-space, nothing was continuous.[7]

Schrödinger's equations did, however, solve one problem. They gave the probability of a particle in a given energy state, offering a certain amount of predictability in the matter. It is still only a probability, however; there is no absolute guarantee as into which energy state a particle will fall. Thus, you could run an experiment exactly the same a hundred times, with exactly the same set-up conditions, and you will not get the same exact result all 100 times. It is like an archer. An expert archer would have a good chance of hitting the bull's-eye, but he would see some of his shots a little off center. An archer with far less skill, in contrast, would have a much wider spread of arrows across the target. The wave equations of the two archers would be said to be different.

Particle movement can now be seen as essentially random, just within certain limits. Each possible route that a particle can take is described by a wave function, and the chance that a certain path will be chosen is the square of that path's wave function. The whole wave equation for a given particle is then the sum of the probabilities of its different end-states, which must add up to exactly 100 percent since you cannot have over a hundred percent possibility of a particle being around. So, if a particle has three possible energy states, with a 25 percent chance of being in the first, and a 60 percent chance of being in the second, then we know its third must have a 15 percent chance; if not, then we start looking for a fourth energy state hiding around somewhere.

This is where the Copenhagen Interpretation comes into play. A particle is neither wave nor particle until it is measured, or in this case that it will take one of these energy states only once it is measured. Look upon it like a hyper kid running randomly around a park. You know he will always be somewhere in that park, but you just don't know exactly where in it he will be until you call, "Stop!" and have him hold onto a tree or other object. He is frozen in place, and you can see where he is. Call, "Go!" and he starts running around the place again.

Remember that energy is always in motion, so it does not quietly sit around in one spot waiting for you to come by and see where it is.

So one interpretation is that a particle is not real until it has been measured, but adding to this problem is the fact that when we measure a given particle, the detectors that we use are also made up of matter, which is made up of its own assemblage of particles, which cannot be real until *they* have been measured. This is a problem that Schrödinger himself mocked with his infamous thought experiment involving a cat in a box that is neither alive nor dead until someone looks inside the box. Additionally, the particles of the detector will interact on some level with what is being detected. This limits how precisely we can measure something.

Chapter 2

THE UNCERTAINTY PRINCIPLE AND ENTANGLEMENT

To measure something we have to interact with it on some level. Try measuring the height of someone without going near the person. Can't be done accurately. Now, hold a measuring tape up next to the person as you tell him or her to hold still, or shine a laser-powered range finder at the person without the laser actually hitting him. Again, it can't be done accurately. This is the problem with measuring the state of an electron. We interfere enough with it to cause it to collapse into one energy state or another, altering it when we try to see if it's there or not. How can we possibly measure its position and momentum if we change them, however slightly, while in the process of doing so?

The Heisenberg Uncertainty Principle

The solution is Heisenberg's Uncertainty Principle. It states that we can never know with absolute precision both the particle's position and momentum at the same instant; it's either one or the other measured exactly, or both with lesser degrees of accuracy. This is stated as

$$xp \geq h/4\pi$$

So, if you determine an object's position with uncertainty (x), there must be an uncertainty in momentum (p) such that uncertainty of position and momentum is greater or equal to Planck's famous constant (h) times 4 times pi (π). Again, you can determine either the position or the momentum of an object as accurately as you like, but the act of doing so makes your measurement of the other property that much less exact.[1]

Let's go back to the kid in the park. He's still running around, but his mother wants to know exactly where he might be running. So again she calls, "Stop," and he freezes in place. She can now determine exactly where he is standing, which direction he's aimed at, and if he was headed toward that bramble-covered wire fence. However, since he *has* stopped, she can no longer tell how fast he was running. Alternatively, she could tell him to keep running around and use a stopwatch to determine how fast he's going, but since his position is constantly shifting as he runs, she is completely unable to determine *exactly* where he is standing at any given moment.

This principle applies to particles, but what about anything else? Because all matter is made up of particles, this principle should to apply to all bulk matter as well. Yet, if we can't measure anything exactly, then how can we know it even really exists? Apparently, we've a few more gaps to fill in.

Another interpretation of the Uncertainty Principle is to compare it to using a ruler. If your ruler is marked off in sixteenths of an inch, then you can't measure anything more precisely than to the nearest sixteenth of an inch. If it is smaller than that, you would only be able to guess within half the distance between the marks on your ruler, but no better than that. You just need a better ruler. Well, the ultimate ruler is a photon. Why? We can't measure half a photon, and we don't have anything smaller, so that's the limit to what we can observe.

Entanglement

Albert Einstein formulated the Theory of Relativity, which basically says that space is curved and there is no absolute, because everything is observed relative to something else. Most importantly, he stated that the fastest speed anything in this universe can go is the speed of light. Not being a fan of quantum mechanics, he spent a good deal of his life after 1925 trying to determine precisely both the position and the momentum of a particle in order to find a violation of the Uncertainty Principle and hence quantum mechanics. In 1935, Einstein and two others proposed an experiment to do just that. The idea was to set up an interaction such that two particles could go off in opposite directions and not interact with anything else. When they are far apart, then scientists could measure the momentum of one and the position of the other. Because of conservation of momentum, you can determine the momentum of the particle not measured, so when you measure others position you know both its momentum and position. The only way quantum physics could be true is if the particles could communicate faster than the speed of light, which Einstein reasoned would be impossible because of his Theory of Relativity.[2]

The experiment was finally carried out in 1982 and it was determined that even if information needed to be communicated faster than light to prevent it, it was not possible to determine both the position and the momentum of a particle at the same time. On the one hand, this does not mean that it's possible to send a message faster than light since viewing either one of the two particles gives no information about the other. It is only when both are seen that we find that quantum mechanics has agreed with the experiment. On the other hand, this doesn't mean that relativity is wrong, just that the particles do not communicate by any means we know about. All we know is that every particle knows what every other particle it has ever interacted with is doing. Even though Einstein did not initially believe in this possibility, he did observe it and referred to it as a "spooky action at a distance".

This odd principle is known as *entanglement*. When a particle has once met with another similar particle, their energy states can become entangled, such that however far apart they are, what happens to one influences the other. So, not only can the measuring of a particle influence its final state, but the act might also influence the state of another particle somewhere else with which it's entangled. This action at a distance is not something that Einstein liked a whole lot because it seems to be almost magical in nature.[3]

I spend a great deal of time near the beach. A friend of mine asked me about entanglement and how particles can communicate faster than the speed of light. I gave some thought to the question while I was completing my daily mediation routine on the sands of an Atlantic shore. The next day I took two pieces of bamboo and stuck them in the sand about 6 feet apart, pressing them down until only the tips of the bamboo were visible. I asked my friend to use a wedge about the size of an i-phone to block the ocean from his bamboo tip. An ocean wave soon followed hitting the two sticks of bamboo; both tops moved at the same time. How could this be? I explained the ocean is something called the *Zero Point Field* (ZPF); the two sticks represented particles. When the wave hit, both sticks moved without delay. This is an illustration of entanglement.

Particles are always connected via this Zero Point Field. There is some sort of subatomic exchange between them in which communication of energy is going constantly back and forth. But all particles are comprised of energy, which brings us to something suggested by the Zero Point Field equations. These equations extend the individual energy fields that each particle has, into a single field that connects all particles; all matter, everywhere, including our thoughts and us (the Ocean). Thusly, only one energy field exists and everything is a part of it, and because everything is entangled within it.

Another example that I like to use to describe entanglement is that of a picture of a large bowl of (Jell-O brand) gelatin with pieces of fruit floating within it. Poke a fork in at one end and try to stab one of the pieces of fruit. It can be done. Now, try to do it without disturbing the entire bowl. Your result will always be the same. Poke one piece of fruit and the entire bowl of gelatin will wiggle, causing all the fruit within it to jiggle around as well. If you're careful, you will be able to lessen how much jiggling goes on, but you'll never eliminate it. Each piece of fruit inside the gelatin will always feel at least a little something.

Now imagine instead of pieces of fruit there is a lifeboat filled with passengers, each able to move on their own. Whenever one moves, the lifeboat starts jiggling, and everyone feels it. They all know without even glancing in his direction that Fred is trying to get more room to sit. They are all entangled with one another inside the boat.

The Zero Point Field is that crowded boat in which we all find ourselves. It constantly interacts with all particles everywhere on a quantum level. Thus, this constant interaction of quantum particles within the Zero Point Field might be the explanation for entanglement, allowing one particle to be in touch with every other particle at any given moment. But, admitting the existence of the Zero Point Field means admitting that all matter everywhere is interconnected and entangled all throughout the cosmos. The energy of any particle can potentially interact with the energy of any other particle. This opens up a wide range of possibilities once you realize this one simple thing.

All matter is comprised of energy, and human beings are matter. Moreover, we have a brain that generates its own energy and its own Electro-Magnetic field. If all Electro-Magnetic fields are interconnected through this Zero Point Field, so must then the energy of our minds and our thoughts be connected. This explains things such as telepathy, where the thoughts of one person can be projected and picked up by another many miles away, This also explains how a strong enough desire can manifest itself into reality. Our thoughts create a movement in this universal field of entanglement, shifting things around in the manner being willed, until an end result comes up that matches up with the thought pattern that was intended (desired).

Since all energy is connected into this Zero Point Field, and all matter is comprised of energy, it follows that every organism everywhere is in perpetual quantum communication via this field as per the Buddhist precept, "We are all connected." This is an ongoing communication by which our thoughts can have a physical effect. In the same way that measuring the state of an object alters the state of that object, we are sort of measuring our world with our thoughts, and by doing so, changing it, and its state. We are the yardstick being held up to the Universe.

The question then is, "Can the ruler do more than just measure? Can we accurately interfere with the experiment?" In science labs around the world, the hard part in measuring something is trying to *keep* your measuring from interfering with the results, so interfering with it is pretty easy. If you've been trying carefully to measure the height of a column of liquid in a beaker and suddenly decide that you want a lot less liquid in that beaker, then all you have to do is tip the beaker over with your ruler. Your mind is like that; ready to tip over your part of the universe to get what you want. The problem simply remains in how to do the tipping.

Our minds (and our consciousness itself) are now seen to be a substance outside our physical bodies. We are a self-aware measuring stick that can detect itself, and this changes *everything*.

Remember the problem with the wave equation? Or how the cat in the box can be neither alive nor dead until someone opens the box? Conscious decision is the tipping point by which the outside influence determines where the outcome lies. The mysteries and contradictions of quantum mechanics now become quite clear once you realize that *thought* is a part of this grand wave equation as well. Thought is a variable that can alter itself. Deliberate intention is the key to making sense out of this mess as well as how to make use of it. Not only then will a wave function collapse into a final result when observed, but the observer will also guide it to where he wants, consciously or subconsciously. We are each a pulsating packet of energy, a superposition of a multitude of atomic states afloat within the universal sea that is the Zero Point Field; but we are aware of our position within it and able to change it at will because thoughts have energy, and no amount of energy exists in this universe independently of anything else.

Which path will a given particle take? Which one do you *want* it to take?

Chapter 3

THE MIND AND
QUANTUM MECHANICS

What is thought and how does it connect up with quantum mechanics? Your brain is comprised of a tight network of nerve cells, all interacting with one another and generating an overall electrical field. This electric field is detectable with standard medical equipment. Your brain waves are simply the superposition of the multitude of electrical states being formed by your nervous system. Not only your brain but also your entire body has an electric field. Any place where there is a nerve cell, there is electricity. It is just concentrated the greatest around your head because that's where the bulk of the nerve cells are. Any time you've felt the shock of static electricity, or used a touch-sensitive screen, you've proven that you have an electric field.

Nothing is mysterious about that part. Being an electric field, it has all of those overlying electric wave patterns that comprise your brain waves. These patterns are governed by the same equations governing the Electro-Magnetic spectrum, light, particles, and everything else in the Universe. The light seen coming from a star and the energy of your mind—these are one and the same type.

Your thoughts, now, are formed in this electric field. The measurable perturbations and disturbances in the brain's overall electric field are your actual thoughts racing through your mind. As you read this book, the thoughts you are thinking of it, and the words your mind is processing, are all electrical impulses that can be measured if you had a few wires hooked up between your head and a machine. So thoughts are energy just like everything else.

This means your thoughts are governed by the rules of both quantum mechanics and Schrödinger's Wave Equations. All those same weird things about quantum mechanics that describe how an electron or photon behave, apply to you and your thoughts as well. Those are the particle-wave duality, the Uncertainty Principle, and entanglement. This implies that, like any other particle-source of energy, we are entangled with everything we've ever encountered, such as the environment around us and the rest of the Universe through the Zero Point Field. We'd mentioned that consciousness is the key to making the mysteries of quantum mechanics work; this is how it happens.

The one difference between a photon and us is that we can think. We are conscious. As such, we can choose which of the possibilities before us we wish to collapse our wave function into. Because we are entangled with our environment, we can affect that as well; influence the randomness, just as it can influence us, but because we are conscious, we can choose what part of the randomness around us to be affected by, and how we in turn would like to affect it. Through entanglement, we can affect change in our environment. Our minds are transceivers, able to receive and send signals into the quantum soup of the Zero Point Field by way of the highly coherent frequencies of our thoughts.

Our thoughts can manifest in our physical reality. This was the whole point of my first book, *The Point of Power*.[1]

I don't just mean vague, seemingly lucky events. History has shown us miracles attributed to saintly people. These things have either been left unexplainable or dismissed as exaggerations. (We'll cover that more in the second section of this book, but for now let's continue with the mind.)

So, why can't you just will yourself into a better life? Well, maybe you can; maybe the mess you're in right now is a result of your conscious or subconscious undermining your efforts with conflicting signals. Have you ever had a long run of bad luck? You get to where you expect more bad things to just happen, and they do. Have you ever had a long run of good luck? When you're on top of the world and honestly feel that nothing can go wrong ... then nothing does. All of these actions are physical manifestations of your thoughts, and that's when you *aren't* even actively trying to change anything!

So you need to be careful. Thoughts attract like thoughts. When you're depressed or angry, more of it just might come your way. Your mood and subconscious desires are putting out signals all the time. If you want to change something, then the problem becomes one of focus. Through our thoughts we can heal or harm ourselves, so it all depends on aligning our thoughts and intentions to direct a clearer signal out to environment and universe around us. Conscious thought harnesses the power of the tiny quantum particles to manifest enormous changes, you only have to make sure that your transmitter is working properly. Meditation is one technique that has been used to bring thought into a clearer focus, and align the waves of your mental energy like light in a laser beam. This puts you more into tune with the Zero Point Field, so that your desires can be better heard and acted upon.

As I spoke to the Monks, they appeared to drift back into a meditative state looking back to the Mala beads to quiet their mind. (Also training their brain to quiet itself). They remained conscious of my interview questions, but went back and forth. It occurred to me that as they quieted their mind to go to a resting state, the background noise that the rest of us continually suffer from is removed leaving a cleaner place from which to pose an intention or simply react to a life situation with right action. How many thoughts from past experiences do we have going on in the background (or possibly in our subconscious as well) that haunt our every move? How many thoughts cause us to question what we are doing, or to doubt ourselves or other humans with whom we are in transaction? This lack of being in a Faith Wave blocks manifestations and sends a confused message to the Universe (or some would say, God).

In *The Point of Power*, I suggest setting an intention the same way you place your order in a restaurant, namely, without doubt as though it has already been prepared and will be delivered as ordered. By clearing out the background noise, you increase the transmission of that intention and its ability to manifest quickly and as you request. "Ask and it shall be given."[2]

Don't forget that besides setting an intention clearly, we need to declare our intention through our behaviors. (Here is where my restaurant order analogy could be misunderstood; the Bible did not mean ask and then just sit there and wait for it.) Manifesting entails visualizing life with the intention already achieved.

The detachment is what requires faith that the universe will cooperate. Hence, we must train the brain to go into Faith Wave. This is the hardest part because you have to let go of your need to control or force, or else you are not in Faith Wave Mode. You are in Ego. The mind needs to emit a proper signal in order for the concepts we hear about in New Age self-help programs to work. This is why often times they do not work.

How powerful of a transceiver is the human mind? A single atom radiates a small Electro-Magnetic Field or EMF. A molecule is comprised of a collection of atoms, so it has an even stronger EMF, and it takes a huge number (we're talking billions, here) of molecules to form a single cell. The human brain has at least 200 million such nerve cells, the whole of which form the collective EMF of your thoughts and your brain waves. This is all part of the collective effort of billions and billions of atoms operating as a single EMF field that are powered by our thoughts and emotions as it reaches out into the larger field of the world around us. This sounds pretty powerful even before sticking active intention behind it.

An undisciplined mind can attract whatever its subconscious might be dwelling on. So, if you become too preoccupied with how bad something is, then you will only tune into and attract more of the same. Emotion is key, for it directs the intention of your thoughts and the quality of the signal that you are broadcasting. A positive attitude will allow you to attract more positive events. Sounding less scientific at this point? Are you ready to tune me out as a snake oil salesman? Well, consider the following.

Your thoughts are like a gravitational field; the more of it there is, the greater the pull on surrounding objects. Gravity is a force that manifests from matter and energy, and, it has weight and mass. Now, your thoughts have weight of a sort; they are a concentration of quantum energy afloat in the endless Zero Point Field. The more of it there is in that concentration, the more it will attract into itself from outside sources. It also has a polarity and will tend to attract that with which it is more in sync. This polarity is governed by your emotional state. The saying "like attracts like" can be taken to the realm of the Zero Point Field.

But let's try a few basic equations to gain some solidity on this. In electricity, there is one given as:

$$P=IV$$

The electrical power (P) generated by a source with a current (I) and voltage (V). This is a physically measurable quantity. Now instantly you may notice one small detail. The brain is an electric field, with a current at a voltage. So, your brain has a measurable amount of electric power. You can stick that quantity into the wave equations in something called *Perturbation Theory* to see what sort of effect you can have on the environment around you. The end result is that thoughts have power, measurable power. It simply remains to see how that power can be used.[3]

The Bose-Einstein Condensate

The Point of Power discusses the Bose-Einstein Condensate. This is an exotic state of matter in which the particles in this Condensate all occupy the same space, becoming as one. This is something usually not allowed by the rule that says no two particles can occupy the same space or the same energy state. It is sort of equivalent to a laser but with matter particles replacing photons; their energies merging to become part of the same whole. This is normally only possible at extremely low temperatures, but recent work has begun applying it to living tissues.[4]

So, a Bose-Einstein Condensate is a lump of matter that is all in the same energy state and working as one. Say the brain is a lump of matter, all of it in the same energy state and working as one. The brain is a condensate generated when the electrical field of thought excites it.

Millions of neurons in the brain maintain coherent thought and work as one structure. Brain waves can be measured on encephalographs where they can be seen to actually be waveform transmissions. Furthermore, the quantum wave function of the brain is not entirely random because it maintains a phase-difference that parallels the duality of the wave and particle. The wave aspect gives us the mental and the particle aspect the material.

This condensate brings order out of chaos, allows us to create reality by interpreting, and manipulates the frequencies of other things in our world of space and time. Is this another exotic theory of physics, or more proof that thought and reality are one and the same? I say both.

Biology

The Point of Power also discusses how biology theory and scientific experiments have been getting into things as well. *Energy Cardiology* is a theory that all biological systems are constantly exchanging information and that such participation alters the exchange. This is exactly like quantum mechanics.[5]

Or take *Neurotheology* (literally, brain-theology). This new field is at the intersection between the brain and the spiritual where functioning brain imaging is used on meditating monks to locate the physical center of the brain responsible for the feeling of "oneness," often felt in deep meditation. Such brain scans have reflected the state of the mind when in such a focus as well as displayed the parts of the brain involved. This is an actual physical measurement of what would be termed a "purely spiritual" experience.

Kinesiology is the study of the effects of feelings and emotions on the well being of your body. Through 29 years of study, it has been found that the human body becomes stronger or weaker with one's mood, so with a simple muscle test the state of your mind can be rated. This has been used to construct a scale to rate the level of one's consciousness. It stands to follow that the higher the level of one's consciousness, the more in tune with the Zero Point Field one is. Hence, the better one is able to use it to manifest one's thoughts into reality. This scale has a direct conversion into *hertz* (a measure of frequency), demonstrating that each of us has a frequency on which we operate and through which energy flows.

All of this is biological support for what used to be thought of as purely spiritual stuff.

Chapter 4

BRAIN WAVES

To see exactly how we can affect our reality through thought alone, we need to know a little about the brain, because that is where all the action is. The brain generates waves, and for our purposes, one (or some combination thereof) is a contender for our Faith Wave.[1]

The hippocampus is the part of the brain that allows us to keep track of our environment, and to form memories. It can also send and receive brain waves of frequencies that might provide a biological and quantum connection with the Zero Point Field. The hippocampus is a part of the limbic system (other components of which are the amygdala, septum, limbic cortex, and fornix). The hippocampus supports a variety of functions including emotion and behavior, and receiving input from various endorphins including serotonin, norepinephrine, and dopamine.

— Serotonin is the happiness hormone.
— Norepinephrine is responsible for triggering the body's fight or flight response.
— Dopamine increases blood pressure and heart rate.
— The frequency of one's brain waves affects how endorphins get sent out.

The brain can generate brain waves of a variety of frequency ranges, labeled as Alpha, Beta, Theta, Delta, and Gamma.[2]

— Delta waves are registered during unconsciousness and fall down to between 0.1 Hz and 4Hz.

— Theta brain waves occur at 4 Hz to 7 Hz and are associated with powerful surges of emotion and states of enhanced creativity, such as daydreaming.

— Alpha waves are lower on the scale and are generated when we're in a state of physical or mental relaxation; they range from 7 Hz (Hertz) to 12Hz.

— Beta waves are the normal range of brain waves used for handling our daily experiences and problems. Our brains use them to keep us alert when we need to tackle problems, or feel anxious or nervous about something. Beta waves trigger the release of the stress hormone dopamine, and range in frequency from 13 Hz to 60 Hz.

— Gamma waves are at the top of the frequency range (though with the lowest amplitude), oscillating from 25 Hz to 100 Hz, with 40 Hz being the average.

Gamma waves are our primary candidate for our Faith Wave. These waves link and process information from all parts of the brain, and are associated with higher levels of intelligence, compassion, self-control, and feelings of happiness. They are also thought to lead to higher levels of consciousness and improved mental focus. Gamma waves also work as a natural antidepressant, trigger the release of hormones to elevate the mood, and increase empathy and compassion.

Note that Beta waves, triggered by stress, lead to the higher frequency Gamma waves, which are responsible for rising above the stress. Beta waves originate in the left side of our brain, whereas Gamma waves are generated across the entire brain.

At a cutoff point, stressful Beta waves are transformed into the calming and peaceful state induced by Gamma waves, like a sudden shifting of gears. Perhaps this is the brain's way of allowing us to rise above a highly stressful situation, so we can have the motivation to continue on, solve our problems, and choose our life's course. Gamma waves lead to improved memory and sensory perception, and are associated with improved learning and reasoning ability. So it might almost make one think that stress is one way to achieving a transcendental state.

Going into Gamma mode allows the brain to better cope with bad situations, but, pain is not the way to higher consciousness. When our brains generate Alpha and Theta waves, Gamma waves are also being created. The generation of Theta and Gamma waves occurs in an alternating fashion. The Beta wave frequency is completely ignored at this moment, implying that stress is not needed to get to those sought-after Gamma waves. What a relief, right?

The generation of Alpha waves amongst other things, prompts the release of the chemical serotonin. This is the link between feeling relaxed, and using our brain to help us connect with the Zero Point Field and manifesting our desires. The release of serotonin has a positive effect on the hippocampus, enabling it to form new memories, have better spatial memory, and an improved mind's eye for layouts of new environments. This is important if you want to accurately envision the dreams that you would like to manifest. Serotonin also affects other areas of the brain including the most important, prefrontal cortex.

The prefrontal cortex is where we store our "what if" thoughts, envision possible rewards for our current activities, and predict future outcomes based on present actions. The prefrontal cortex is the control center of the brain. So, as we can see, the hippocampus and pre-frontal cortex are essential for maintaining a strong connection to the Zero Point Field and clearly manifesting our own reality.

To manifest such desires however, our brains need to remain healthy and happy to perform as efficiently as possible, which means serotonin and more Alpha waves. Serotonin has quite a large effect on both our mental and physical health.

The hippocampus contains high levels of special receptors—making it more vulnerable to long-term stress than any other part of the brain. There is even some evidence that people who have experienced severe long-lasting stress or depression show a significant decrease in the size and efficiency of the hippocampus. This is significant in that a reduction in the hippocampus' size also appears to be related to a reduction in the number of serotonin receptors. Serotonin then, is the chemical basis for keeping our minds happy and healthy enough to induce the range of brain waves responsible for positive thinking, and positive thinking is essential for connecting up with the Zero Point Field to manifest our desires.

Alpha brain waves have been linked to higher levels of self-respect, a less obsessive-compulsive attitude to achieving perfection, a decrease in the fear of failure, an increase in passion, and an overall improved sense of satisfaction, with better physical health and vitality. In other words, Alpha waves offer a certain level of detachment toward manifesting your desired goals. Alpha waves are also said to engender a certain sense of being "connected" while they lessen feelings of loneliness. Perhaps it allows us to be connected with others entangled into the Zero Point Field.

Faith Wave

So what about our Faith Wave? *Faith Wave* is a superposition of brain waves fueled mainly by the Gamma, and formed by lower resonances from the Alpha and Theta, which act like a pair of bookends to keep the Gamma from toppling off the bookshelf of your mind. Why these waves?[3]

Higher levels of Gamma waves are known to improve memory, sharpen the five senses, and bind your memory and senses together, like when a certain smell reminds you of events from a certain memorable night. Gamma waves are also linked with the ability to process large amounts of information in a relatively short time. People with high levels of Gamma have sharp memories, are quick learners, and with that sensory-memory link are quite adept at visualizing a smell or sound in their minds.

Theta waves are associated with the old "learning while you sleep", daydreaming, sleep dreaming, creativity, and relaxation. In fact, too much Theta activity is behind such conditions as attention-deficit disorders; and lack of mental focus, which is why you need a bit of Alpha around to balance it out, thus the reason that Alpha and Theta are the mental bookends for our Gamma wave state. It is interesting to note that children have the highest levels of Theta activity, and are more carefree and less stressed out than adults. Theta waves have also been linked with intuition, learning, and a strong connection to your subconscious.

Notice the possible pattern here: Gamma and Theta are visual sensory-memories, sharp memories, and creativity. It would seem that this adds up to something, and it does. This is something simple and something that children have in abundant supply, yet something that is all too often frowned upon in certain walks of adult life: Imagination. Yes, the key to generating your Faith Wave is as simple as stretching your imagination.

Lose yourself to flights of fancy every so often. Let your imagination soar, and you will drop the stress that limits you. Increase the Gamma and Theta waves that you induce and put yourself in a better state to access the Zero Point Field, and affect change through the power of your thoughts. And when exercising your imagination, just as kids so often do, where are your pre-programmed mental limits? They are *gone* and, with them, whatever holds you back from manifesting your desires.

The difference between you and a child is that a child is too young and untrained to have yet developed the mental focus and discipline to aim his or her intentions anywhere. An adult has this discipline, but has lost touch with his or her imagination in favor of "facing the realities of life." Reality is what you will, and imagination is the key to your Faith Wave, if you have the discipline, or better yet, the openness and the grace to follow it.

I would also add in one additional thing: people in the Theta range have a stronger emotional connection with themselves. They also experience stronger degrees of whatever emotion they happen to be feeling at the time. This tendency can be both a good and a bad thing depending on the emotion in question. Let's think positive: kick that nasty Ego out the door, and focus on stronger connections with our good feelings.

Back to observing ourselves as children: When in the throws of unbridled creative imaginings, what type of emotion do you think that children are experiencing? Enthusiasm. They have an excitement for whatever they imagine, which is another trait that is too often pressed out of them by adulthood. Yet, this would appear to be another key because when you are excited about something—when your heart is in it—then you *know* with absolute certainty that it will happen. And when you are in such a state, where is the fear? The doubt? The worry? Where are the limits? They become what they have always been, a fog dispersing upon the winds.

So, while the instrumentation of science now tells us that our Faith Wave is the Gamma waveform bolstered by Theta and Alpha waves, we can more commonly view this equation as imagination plus focus plus Faith (positive emotions, absolute certainty, and enthusiasm for an endeavor) equals Faith Wave. Here is our key to generating it.

How capable are our minds to hook up to the Zero Point Field depends on how pliable our brain is when it comes to finding and transmitting the desired signals or frequencies. Maybe it's only possible when we're children since after all our minds are still expanding? Or, maybe there is still something more about the brain that allows it a certain amount of flexibility even well into adulthood. If so, then this flexibility is the key to this whole subject. This flexibility has recently taken on a new term and field of study called Neuroplasticity.

Chapter 5

NEUROPLASTICITY

Not long ago, neuroscientists perceived the brain—once it got past a certain age—as fixed and immutable. The first transition from peak state was thought to occur after adolescence: The brain was in the final shape and structure and would remain in that state ever after or decline from then until death.

More recently, the age limit was thought to be about one's mid-20s before the brain hardened into place like drying cement. Beyond this age, the brain would be incapable of growing any new patterns of neurons, and therefore, the brain was hardwired into place.

Several observations seemed to vouch for this conclusion. For instance, if someone lost his or her sight, then that person's visual cortex would go dark, or if someone lost feeling in an arm, then the part of the brain corresponding to that area would similarly go silent. Only in childhood could the brain expand and restructure itself.

Dreams were assumed to last only a brief fraction of a second. Evidence came from various sources, such as one man's dream that he was being guillotined. His bed's headboard happened to fall and bang him on the head and because this "cause" took only a brief moment, then complete and vivid dreams must occur only in a fraction of a second.

Modern neuroscience now takes a different view and questions these anecdotes and assumptions. Studies involving brain scans of meditating monks have shown how much older monks still have more pliable minds that are able to adapt and restructure themselves. Such a trait is essential in training oneself in manifesting reality through our contact with the Zero Point Field.

Plasticity

The brain has a certain amount of plasticity throughout its life as illustrated in the prior section. When you learn something, a new neuron is there to record it. New neural pathways lay down and old ones are rearranged to make this neuron recoverable.[1]

A new fixation was theorized. In the basic structure of the brain, the section that performs each type of function was thought to be fixed and immutable by adulthood. It was thought that a given section of the brain could only perform a given function and never take over for anything else that may need help. If a cluster of neurons were ever damaged, then there would never be anymore new ones to replace them. You were stuck with what you had, which included your intelligence, your memory capacity, and your creative power. All of them were thought to be fixed into place.

Over the last couple of decades, evidence has been slowly mounting that this is not so. Yes, the brain may be on more of a rush to expansion during childhood as children learn new things when their creative imaginations are at their peak, but how many people are still in school learning new things after about the age of twenty-five, and how many adults still really engage their creative imaginations?

It is now known that when a section of the brain is damaged, that other regions can take over. The brain can rewire itself around the damaged area to pick up the slack. The brain reorganizes itself as needed, but for these new connections to take place, the neurons must be stimulated through proper activity. Undamaged axons can grow new nerve endings to hook up with neurons whose links were damaged, or connect with other undamaged neurons to form entirely new neural pathways to accomplish what is needed.[2]

In 1923, Karl Lashley found evidence that the brain of a rhesus monkey remained fairly malleable even in adults with neurons making different paths for the same stimuli from week to week.

Then, in the 1970s, Michael Merzenich severed nerve endings in the hands of adult monkeys only to find that the monkeys' brains rewired to continue to use the corresponding part of the brain that should have then gone dark from the lack of stimuli from the severed nerve. The brain had begun to process signals from other parts of the hand where the monkey could still feel.

Stroke victims used to be consigned to limited use of the affected limb for the rest of their lives, yet now it is quite standard for physical therapy to re-strengthen the neural pathways that govern use of that limb and allow a victim to regain its full use as the brain rewires itself, grows new neural connections and repairs old ones. Even victims of stroke that had been paralyzed for years, were found to be able to recover through the use of brain-stimulating exercises. Such discoveries have led to the motivational therapies that are in use today.

While brain plasticity was well documented as occurring before the critical period that ended brain development after childhood, neuroscientist Michael Merzenich argued that brain plasticity could occur well beyond the critical period. He has been a pioneer in the field of brain plasticity for over thirty years, claiming that brain exercises may be as good as drugs to rehabilitate someone from diseases such as schizophrenia, and that improvements in cognitive functioning are possible even in elderly people.[3]

His first proof of adult plasticity came during a postdoctoral study with Clinton Woosley that focused on observations of what happens in the brain when one peripheral nerve is cut and later regenerated. The two micro-mapped the cortical sections of the monkeys' brains corresponding to use of their hands before and after cutting a peripheral nerve, and sewing the ends together. The hand map in the brain was expected to be jumbled and disorganized, but instead it was found to be nearly normal. Based on that, Merzenich decided that "if the brain map could normalize its structure in response to abnormal input, the prevailing view that we are born with a hardwired system had to be wrong. The brain had to be plastic."

Strokes have been induced in monkeys in laboratory experiments, damaging select portions of the brain that correspond to some form of movement and hence the loss of the use of one limb. It was found in these experiments that if adjacent areas of the brain were stimulated then the paralyzed limb would move once again. Other such experiments have confirmed the ability of the brain to repair itself in regions long thought to be irreparable. Nerve cells could die, but they can now grow anew.

Neuroplasticity lies in the brain as a whole and not just its separate parts. Yes, nerve cells can regrow when once it was thought that they could not, but as we scale things up it has been found that entire regions of the brain are able to reorganize and take on the functions of adjacent damaged sections. It is the brain itself, operating as a whole, that is able to mold and manipulate itself as the need arises. The brain is constantly creating and pruning neural connections based on sensory input, frequency of use of a given connection, and efficiency of a given connection.

To give you an idea of the complexity of the brain, at birth each neuron starts off with about 2,500 connections. By age two or three a child's sensory stimulation and environmental experience have boosted each neuron's connections to around 15,000 synapses. By the time we enter adulthood, this number declines a bit as the ineffective and rarely used connections are pruned away. Neuroplasticity is at its peak in childhood, but that does not mean it goes entirely away.

In fact, the more pliable one's brain is, the better he is able to learn something. Our ability to learn and recall information depends on the number of synapses that devote themselves to recording this piece of information. The more plastic one's brain, the more interconnections can form and as a result the better one is able to learn and recall. If the brain had no plasticity at all, then it would be unable to learn.

So, if the brain has a certain amount of pliability in one regard, then it stands to reason that there may be more of it elsewhere, such as when reorganizing itself to recover from an injury, as previously mentioned. After all, what is the difference between learning a new fact and trying to recover an old one? Learning how to ski, for instance, requires your brain to record what set of neurons to fire off when, and which muscles to stimulate at the proper times. Learning how to walk again after a stroke requires the brain to figure out which set of neurons to fire off to take that first step, and how to signal the muscles to do the required job. Both instances require the brain to form new connections, and find a place in its structure to record this new information of movement. From the point of view of learning, both examples are exactly the same. There is no difference at all between learning a new skill and recovering an old one.

How plastic one's brain is, therefore, determines how difficult or easy such rewiring will be. Taking advantage of the brain's plasticity, programs are being developed to help treat learning difficulties. Michael Merzenich developed a computer program known as "FastForWord" that gives seven brain exercises to help with the language and learning problems associated with dyslexia. Another study was done in experimental training to see if it could be used to help recover cognitive function lost to old age; the result of that study was the conclusion that such a brain program taking advantage of brain plasticity could offer notable results. Both of these examples demonstrate the brain's ability to rewire itself to recover lost function from injury and age.[4]

But, what if the brain is not injured and you try to take advantage of its plasticity? Can you actually improve beyond the original design parameters? Experiments with monkeys and implanted devices have shown that this can be true. In experiments lasting a day each, a monkey is implanted with an electronic connection from the motor cortex of its brain to an actuator. At first, the monkey is trained to move the actuator by moving a joystick while the machines record the neurons firing off in his brain. Later, control of the actuator is switched from the joystick movement to the activity in the monkey's brain occurring while the monkey is operating the joystick. The result was that the monkey learned to control the actuator with the power of his thoughts alone. It was a new limb in the form of the actuator, not the relearning of an old limb.

This was a pretty basic experiment with some potential for the future, but what if we step it up from monkeys a bit? The ability of humans to take advantage of the plasticity of our brains and work in some improvements can be evidenced in the meeting of science and meditation.

Meditation and Neuroplasticity

The Dalai Lama is the world's leader of Tibetan Monks and an international figurehead for meditation. Following my interviews in Bejing China while living amongst the Monks in the Lama Temple I returned to the States. I then sought out a an audience with the Dalai Lama himself. After a short delay and several requests I was granted a short interview with him. We discussed how the mind, body, and brain interact. I wondered whether the the mind could actually change the way the brain worked. Could consciousness effect the brain? I was surprised at his sincere interest in explaining things that he knew to be true from his studies and experience as a monk. I was impressed that we both insisted on scientific collaboration.

To put the question more directly: In addition to the brain giving rise to thoughts, hopes, beliefs, and emotions that add up to this thing we call the mind, does the mind also act back on the brain to cause physical changes in the very matter that created it? If so, then pure thought would change the brain's activity, its circuits or even its structure."

The Dalai Lama affirmed the idea that mind can indeed act back upon the brain. Thus, not only is our brain plastic enough to keep adapting, but we can *choose* how to sculpt our minds. This supposition has also led to the discovery by others that neuroplasticity cannot occur without attention. So, if a skill becomes part of your routine—so that you can do it nearly automatically, such as walking—then practicing it will no longer change the brain. And if you take up mental exercises to keep your brain young, then they won't be as effective should you find yourself able to do them without paying much attention. Like any good exercise, you need to change it up every so often.

Researcher Michael Merzenich found that the method we choose to sculpt our minds has actual, physical, and measurable changes etched within our brains. Practices such as meditation and Chi Gong can keep the old mental circuits active and form new ones, leading to a cycle of continual self-improvement. Of course, practitioners of meditation have been saying this for centuries.

Professor Richard Davidson of the University of Wisconsin in Madison has been working with the Dalai Lama and his Buddhist monks for quite some time, hooking some of them up to machines to see how their brain waves differ from those of student volunteers. In such experiments, 8 monks and 10 volunteers are wired up to an electroencephalograph to record their brain waves. The volunteers had no previous experience in meditating, save a quick crash course as they walked in the door. The type of meditation used is called "non-referential compassion," and involves the meditator focusing on unlimited compassion and loving kindness toward all living beings. The monks, on the other hand, had decades of experience in the practice. The researchers chose this type of meditation because it focuses on a transformed state of being instead of concentrating on particular objects, memories, or images.[5]

As the student volunteers meditated, their brain waves began to alter, specifically their Gamma waves showed a slight, but significant increase. For the monks, their Gamma signal kept rising throughout the exercise, which was not surprising given their greater experience with the practice. What was surprising is that, in between the meditation sessions when the monks were at rest, their Gamma signals never fell. Even when not meditating, the monks' brain waves displayed increased activity associated with perception, problem solving, and consciousness. Furthermore, the more hours of meditation a monk had under his belt, the stronger his Gamma signal, or his Faith Wave. This sort of response—that higher doses of a drug or activity lead to a greater effect than for lower levels—is what researchers look for to determine a positive cause and effect. This proved to Davidson that mental training could instill lasting traits into the brain.

Subjects had the most activity in the areas of the brain that handle emotions, positive feelings, and planned movements. Meanwhile, regions that keep track of what is "Self versus Other" quieted down. Moreover, the areas in the monks' brains that underlie empathy and maternal love had much stronger connection from the frontal to the emotional regions; the pathway used by higher thought to control emotions. The most dramatic changes occurred in monks with the most experience in meditation, showing that meditation makes it easier for the brain to activate its compassion neural circuits ... easier for the brain to generate its *Faith Wave*. According to Davidson, such findings clearly indicate that meditation can change the function of the brain in a lasting way.

Thus, the brain is plastic enough not just to repair itself but also to improve itself as well. Even if you are long past the years of childhood, you are still capable of altering your neurophysiology enough to display noticeable improvements that can affect the way you think, the way you feel, and the overall efficiency of your brain activity. Such improvements lead to a more focused brain and a better ability to call out to the cosmos and the Zero Point Field to manifest your desires. We know now that you can change yourself, in actual physically measurable ways, and that the brain can then adapt to accomplish what you need it to do. We also now know that part of the secret is being aware of what you are doing because routine actions do not engender change. The brain will change to adapt and perform, and if you can change yourself, then you are taking the first step to inducing change upon your environment. The brain, like any lump of matter, is entangled with the Zero Point Field, so it stands to reason that if it can change itself then it can certainly change that with which it is entangled.

To put things in a more poetic way, the more faith you have—in you and your part in the world—the better things will be, and the easier it will be to generate this faith and change. Like any skill, it gets better with practice. And for this, the best example we can cite is to look once again at children. Their brains are still pliable because of their youth, of course, and because they have not yet learned to limit themselves. No longer young? Okay, in your physical age this may be the case, yet, you have the possibility of making or keeping your mind pliable. How? By exercising your mind through imagination and unbridled flights of fancy, focusing on what you *can* do instead of what you *can't*. The natural plasticity of the brain will manifest itself.

Experiments with rats at the University of California, Berkeley, have shown that when they are placed in enriched environments with lots of stimuli and challenges, levels of a brain enzyme associated with learning and memory actually increased, as did the number of synapses, brain proteins, and the weight of their brains; specifically, the density of those sections of the brain associated with thinking, learning, and memory. These structural changes took place almost immediately following their introduction into enriched environments.[6]

The rats got smarter. And if a rat can do it, then I'm sure that humans are more than capable. In essence, you can think yourself smarter and more capable.

We now have the final piece of the biological part of the puzzle. We know how the brain operates, what it takes to connect to the Zero Point Field, and how manifestation is started. Now we need more information on the nature of the Zero Point Field itself.

Chapter 6

THE ZERO POINT FIELD

The Zero Point Field (ZPF) has been discussed in the prior chapters. Yet, it is such a vital component to activating Faith Wave that it needs to be discussed in a more holistic way. So, let's start with the basics. What is known about the ZPF and how did its discovery come about?

ZPF Basics

In Quantum Field Theory, the Vacuum State is the quantum state with the lowest possible energy; it contains no physical particles and is the energy of the ground state. This is also called the *zero point energy*; the energy of a system at a temperature of absolute zero. But quantum mechanics says that, even in their ground state, all systems still maintain fluctuations and have an associated zero point energy as a consequence of their wave-like nature. Thus, even a particle cooled down to absolute zero will still exhibit some vibration.

Let's consider Liquid Helium-4. Under atmospheric pressure, even at absolute zero, it does not freeze solid and will remain a liquid. This is because its zero point energy is great enough to allow it to remain as a liquid, even if a very cold one. Everything everywhere has Zero Point Energy, from particles to Electro-Magnetic fields, and any other type of field. Combine them all together, and you have the vacuum energy or the energy of all fields in space.

This would seem to imply that a Vacuum State, or simple vacuum, is not empty at all, but the ground state energy of all fields in space. This may collectively be called the Zero Point Field. This Vacuum State contains, according to quantum mechanics, fleeting Electro-Magnetic waves and virtual particles that pop into and out of existence at a whim.[1]

So, we must then ask, can this energy be measured or even calculated? In physics there is something called the Casmir Effect. In this experiment, two unchanged plates are brought together parallel to each other, in a magnetic field. The cavity between the plates cannot sustain all frequency modes of the Electro-Magnetic field, particularly the wavelengths comparable to the plate separation. This creates a zero-point pressure on the outside of the plates which pushes the plates together, much like how radiation pressure from the Sun pushes a comet's tail away from its nucleus. The resulting effect is called the Casmir Force, and this force increases in strength the closer the plates get, until the plates make actual physical contact or when the plates are so close together that zero-point wavelengths no longer see a perfectly conducting surface.[2]

This Casmir Effect is often sited as evidence of a sea of zero point energy throughout the universe. Another possible manifestation of the ZPF might be the Cosmological Constant so often used in cosmology; some say it might be a measure of this zero point energy. One calculation even puts the energy of a cubic centimeter of empty space at around a trillionth of an erg; not much, but collect that over all of space and you still get infinity.

In 1913, Albert Einstein and Otto Stern performed an analysis of the specific heat of hydrogen at low temperatures and discovered the available data would best fit if the vibrational energy is one-half of the non-absolute zero state:

$E = 0.5\ hv$

Energy (at absolute zero) equals one-half times Plank's constant (h) times the vibration (v). A much longer equation is used, but at absolute zero, the first term drops out as zero. This is the zero point energy for hydrogen, and space being filled with the stuff that alone would fill the vacuum with zero-point Electro-Magnetic radiation.[3]

Another derivation of the ZPF comes, as mentioned before, from the Uncertainty Principle. For a given particle, one cannot know both its position and momentum at the same time, with the least possible uncertainty being proportional to Planck's constant. This uncertainty relates to the inherent quantum fuzziness of energy and matter due to their wave-like nature. Thus, one cannot have a particle lying motionless at the bottom of its potential well, for then you would know both its position and energy with absolute certainty, so the lowest possible energy of a given system must be greater than the minimum potential of the well; its zero point energy. This leads us to postulate the collective potential of all particles everywhere with their individual zero-point energies merging into one universal Zero Point Field.

Indeed, zero point energy keeps popping up throughout physics. For the ground state of a harmonic oscillator, its zero point energy is called its "expectation value" for its vacuum energy. In Quantum Perturbation Theory, there are terms that are contributions due to vacuum fluctuations, or zero point energy. In Quantum Field Theory, the fabric of space is said to consist of a variety of fields, such as the Electro-Magnetic field, with the field at every point in space and time being a quantum harmonic oscillator interacting with neighboring oscillators, creating a field of energy throughout the vacuum of space.

Back to the Uncertainty Principle. It is said that its basic equation, expressed as:

$$\Delta E \, \Delta t \geq \hbar$$

The change in energy (delta E) times the change in time (delta t) is greater than or equal to Plank's constant. A particle pair with that energy may be spontaneously created for a short time equal to the time factor in this same equation. In fact, virtual particles walk hand in hand with the definition of a vacuum in physics.

From whichever angle you come at it, even a "vacuum" is never empty. It is always filled with energy, fleeting Electro-Magnetic waves, and particles that can pop into and out of existence. This whole collective is the zero point energy of the Universe; the Zero Point Field.

Tapping the ZPF

So with the existence of this ZPF, the question sooner or later arises as to how one can tap it for power. Can such a physical device even be built, or has anyone yet attempted this feat? Some have tried, many of them fakes and frauds trying to get a bit of extra coin by cheating the public, one stands head and shoulders above the crowd. There is one undisputed king of all Electro-Magnetic things. His name invokes equal measures of a scientist and a wizard: Nicola Tesla.[4]

But let's first discuss a bit of background. When Maxwell derived his famous equations for the Electro-Magnetic spectrum, his expression of them was different than their expression today. Prior to calculus, an old branch of mathematics was known as *quaternions*. In this form, the expressions contained extra scalar terms as well as the vector terms that we know of today. At the advent of calculus, converting into this new form meant that the scalar terms were dropped by later scientists. By doing this, however, we missed a whole different aspect of the Electro-Magnetic spectrum.

The classical Electro-Magnetic wave that we know of today is a transverse wave with the electric and magnetic fields oscillating perpendicular to one another along the direction of the wave's propagation. Transverse waves travel through three-dimensional space and weaken with distance. The now missing part of Maxwell's equations suggest that energy can also travel as longitudinal waves as well, and possibly at speeds faster than light. They are like sound waves and oscillate in the direction of their propagation. This scalar wave travels in the time domain and does not weaken with distance. The energy of scalar waves can be tapped by converting them into the more standard transverse vector waves. This is accomplished by the meeting of one scalar wave with its out-of-phase counterpart so they destructively interfere with one another, creating the transverse wave. Correspondingly, a scalar wave can be created by the meeting of two transverse waves that are 180 degrees out-of-phase with each other.

There is a known flux of virtual photons between a dipole and the vacuum; these are actually scalar waves. They can travel immense distances with no loss of energy, and can be created by a dipole, battery, generator, and a permanent magnet with two poles—basically, any sort of dipole in the universe, from an atom to a star. Scalar waves fill the Universe with their abundant energy, the pulse of zero point energy.

But can it be tapped? Back to Tesla for that answer. Nikola Tesla used induction coils to create scalar waves and conducted many experiments where he sent scalar waves around the Earth with no loss in strength. He could send them any distance with practically no loss of energy. Tesla believed this inexhaustible source of energy could be tapped for any use imaginable and came up with designs for both destructive and beneficial devices. His devices envisioned the ability to modify the weather. Negatively to create earthquakes, hurricanes, and tornados or positively to permit the tapping of free energy, anti-gravity propulsion, and curing of any disease by time-reversing the illness. Even today, there are a few experimentalists making their own versions of such devices. At least one of these, the Patterson Power Cell, is being taken seriously enough to be studied at four different universities.

Or, there is John Hutchinson of Vancouver, Canada, who among other such devices, has developed a battery that generates 18 volts at 250 mA and recharges itself from zero point energy. There are many that claim the U.S. military has developed its own secret projects in this field as well.

Back in 1982, the zero point energy appears to have been measured as current noise inside a resistively shunted Josephson Junction, with a frequency of 500 Giga Hertz, by Robert H. Koch, D. J. van Harlingen, and John Clarke of the University of Berkley.[5]

The first thing reputable scientists will say about such free-energy devices is that they violate the laws of thermodynamics. Because the zero point energy is the minimum energy state below which no thermodynamic system can go, then none of this energy can be withdrawn without altering the system to one with a lower zero point energy. Proponents of ZPF free energy point out that because it is the vacuum that is being tapped, no such violation occurs. Thus, physics goes merrily on its way. Statistical invariance implies that the energy density must increase exponentially with frequency. When you integrate over all frequencies, this gives you an infinite energy density. So, theoretically, if you extract a given amount of energy from such a system, you would still have infinite energy density remaining evenly distributed in all directions of the field.

The controversy still exists as to whether it is possible, but the point is that the possibility is there on a theoretical basis, and on a practical basis, people *are* fabricating experimental devices to tap this infinite energy field.

The ZPF Encodes Information

Albert Einstein said that energy can be neither created nor destroyed. Quantum mechanics extends that to *information*, which also can be neither created nor destroyed. In the infinite quantum soup that is the ZPF, as particles exchange energy with one another, they also thus exchange information. After all, what is the ultimate carrier of information? How does your computer, for instance, store and manage information? It does so by the storage and exchange of electrons.

Any particle will do actually, we just happen to use electrons because it works easiest for our technology, but any particle can store information by just being present, and since particles are made up of photons, which are the base unit of energy, then energy itself can store information, and by extension the energy field of the universe, which is the ZPF.

So what sort of energy is stored? Everything that passes through it, which is to say, everything there is. This information is constantly passed back and forth from one particle to another, vibrating across the energy fields of the universe. Like a neighborhood gossip; as something new develops, everyone in the neighborhood hears about it. And like information stored on a computer, it is not merely stored but can be altered by interaction of the surrounding electronics of the universe. Cause and effect are intertwined. Physical reality then, arises from, and is recorded upon, the background energy of the vacuum of space.

Where do we as thinking creatures come into play? People are made of matter, which is a collection of particles, which in turn are made up of quantum-sized packets of energy. So it follows that the particles that comprise a person are in constant communication not only with the rest of the matter that makes up that person but also with the surroundings of said person. Human beings are bundles of energy constantly exchanging information with the ZPF of the universe. If you want it to happen or not; if you are intentionally asking the universe for anything or not—you are in constant communication with everything.

This communication is not just one-way. As the universe contains the self-updating blueprint for whom and what we are, it can both alter and be altered. Quantum information from the ZPF can come into our beings and manifest changes, but we—or any other living thing—can also communicate out into the ZPF to alter what we need to change. The field determines us, and we determine it.

This sounds like entanglement and communication takes place without needing time as a reference point. During my morning runs along Lake Michigan, I cut a path next to the wake line of the last wave. Sometimes I step in the water. Almost automatically, I quickly respond by pulling my shoe out in a split second. No matter how quickly I pull my foot out of the water, my sock is 100 percent drenched causing me to finish my run squeaking along. This is a bad example of entanglement because there is a fractional time delay for my sock to become soaked whereas the two entangled particles have instant interaction. However, I liked the story as it is an illustration of how quickly data (water) energy can be moved to all parts of a subsystem (my wet foot). It certainly seems as instantaneous as it could be, yet with entangled particles there is no time delay what so ever. In fact, there is no such thing as time in the Zero Point field, but let's look at that subject in a few more paragraphs.

Is there proof of such an information exchange emanating from humans via the Zero Point Field? Or is it even something that *can* be proved? Some scientists have obtained evidence enough to show that living things emit a weak radiation and that this radiation may play a crucial part in biological processes, including how certain cells communicate with one another.

German physicist Fritz-Albert Popp has found that humans emit a weak field of highly coherent light, and that one source of this field of light is the strands of DNA in our bodies. It is tied to life itself and could be the auras that some people say they can see around others.[6]

Some French scientists have even shown that they can record the frequency of a molecule, play it to another molecule, and watch as the signal alone takes the place of the molecule itself in starting certain chemical reactions. The fact that chemical reactions alone occur because of colliding molecules has always been dependent on chance and requiring time, more time than is needed for the speed of such biological reactions as anger, fear, or sadness. There are even some scientists working on the notion that some of the brain's functions have to do with an interaction between itself and the ZPF.

Possibly some of the brain's communications with its body may be in terms of waves instead of chemical impulses alone. By one means or another, our brains may be reading and writing information to the ZPF on a quantum level. A few scientists even theorize that our memories live more within the surrounding ZPF than in our heads and that our brains are simply the computer terminal we use to access the mainframe of the ZPF.

Have you ever known something was true, but had no reference point, no factual data to support your sureness? How do you know it is true? This happens to me: I have never read a book or listened to a teacher, yet as I read some of the works published by Carl Jung, Albert Einstein, and others, I felt deep in my gut what was a truth and what may have been manufactured by someone's ego. This gut feeling jumped out at me over and again when reviewing religious texts. I felt like I was accessing the ZPF mainframe and it was giving me hints as I did my research.

The ZPF and Time Dependence

The evidence is mounting that the ZPF is literally timeless—that past, present, and future flow together within the infinite energy field.

Physicist Helmut Schmidt conducted a number of experiments that delve into the timelessness of the ZPF. In one experiment, he sent people to random locations, and then asked them to photograph the locations within 15 minutes of arriving. Afterward, they were asked to fill in a questionnaire that he gave them. Schmidt then asked many clairvoyants to describe all locations involved—before the other people arrived, which they did correctly. Well over 300 experiments later, Schmidt concluded that time and space do not exist for the ZPF in the way that we understand it.[7]

In another experiment Schmidt later conducted, he sent test subjects home with a tape of computer beeps that were randomly arranged to play in the left or right ear. He asked them to focus on influencing whether the beeps played more in one ear than the other. As a control, he kept a copy of each tape for himself, and then only later played it back when his test subjects returned with their results. Not only were the people able to influence which ear the beeps played in but Schmidt's own copies of the tapes also played the exact same sequence. His only conclusion was that the subjects had to have influenced how the beeps were played as the computer was recording them, which is only possible if the ZPF connecting the subjects with their environment does not care about temporal constraints.

Another experiment at Harvard University recreated a scene from 1959. The scene was complete with furniture, films of the day, and period newspapers. Then, the experimenter asked a group of 70 year-olds to live there for a few days. Within a week, all were showing signs of the reversal of their symptoms of aging; increased flexibility, improved eyesight, and improved joints. Their bodies had begun to physically adapt to the mental imagery given them of 1959 when the subjects were a lot younger. One possible explanation is they had connected up with the blueprint of themselves inscribed upon the ZPF from 1959.

The ZPF shows no difference between perceived information and actual information, or between the real and the imagined. Information is information. The brain can retrieve it all the same. The memory of it, of everything, is stored within the ZPF, waiting to be retrieved. It is just as simple as recalling anything else. Do you wish to manifest something for someone else? It is also simple, and something that has been researched as well. This may well explain the peculiar phenomena of people in hospitals who heal quicker when random people around the world pray for them.

The Quantum Hologram

The *quantum hologram* is the name given to the eternal information exchange. The event history of all macroscopic matter is continually broadcasted non-locally and received by other matter in its environment in some cases actually interacting with it. It is the macro-scaled extension of the quantum-level emission and absorption that gives rise to particle entanglement.[8]

Researchers investigating improvements to functional MRI (magnetic resonance imaging) found that the emission and re-absorption of energy by macroscopic-level physical objects carries information about the event history of that object. It does so in the phase differences of the interference patterns of the emitted quanta of energy. The theoretical model for this is the exact same one as used in holography, and so it was termed quantum holography. This provides an explanation for how the whole of a creature learns, adapts, and evolves into self-organized node in a holistic system, and allows for the non-local exchange of information at all scales. It happens at the ultra-microscopic scale, and also at all temperatures.

Entanglement may be the way that individual particles can exchange information in a non-local way, but now quantum holography is present to scale this up, to allow the interaction of molecules and macro-scaled objects and creatures with the Zero Point Field. Individual particles are entangled with the ZPF, but now we see that objects, comprised of a large number of individual particles, can act as a single unit to exhibit its net influence into the ZPF. Thus, this model provides the final connection between people and the Zero Point Field. It is this final connection that can allow science to now deal with the metaphysical, and with such issues as metaphysics, parapsychology, mysticism and religion.

Chapter 7

THE ZPF AND MASS

Just when you think that science is finished being bizarre, something else comes up. Mass itself may be an illusion brought about by the presence of the ZPF. This idea goes back a few decades and has been brought up again by researchers Bernard Haisch, Alfonso Rueda, and H. E. Puthoff in their article in *The Sciences* December 1994 issue.[1]

Einstein said that mass can be converted into energy in his famous equation $E=mc^2$. But, while the equation may be correct, the interpretation of it may be a little off. It may actually detail how much energy is required to give the *appearance* of a given amount of mass, which is a fine-point, but significant distinction.

The ZPF finds no such thing as mass. There is electric charge and energy, which give us the illusion of mass once the presence of the ZPF is taken into account. If the physical universe is comprised entirely of massless electric charges swimming in an infinite sea of energy, then the appearance of mass comes from the interaction of those charges with this universal field of energy. Everything you think of as solid, everything that has mass and inertia—all of this is purely the result of interactions between charges and Electro-Magnetic field.

For some physicists, this idea has the advantage of being able to finally solve one fundamental problem; how to unify the force of gravity with the rest of Nature's fundamental forces. These fundamental forces are gravity, the Electro-Magnetic force, the weak force (responsible for nuclear decay), and the strong force (needed to hold the atom together). The Electro-Magnetic and weak forces have already been shown to be two manifestations of the same thing. They very well might bring in the strong force as well, but gravity has been difficult. Yet, if this new idea is correct, then as mass would arise from the Electro-Magnetic force, so would gravity that stems from that mass.

Mass

So, what is mass? Mass has inertia and gives rise to gravitation. Galileo defined inertia as that which keeps an object of matter in uniform motion, once propelled by a force, until said force stops. Newton put this into the form of his own famous equation, F=ma (Force equals mass times acceleration). So, inertial mass is the resistance an object provides against being moved. Eliminate the force, and the object stops accelerating, and proceeds at a uniform velocity. The ability of an object to resist acceleration is an intrinsic property of all matter.[2]

Newton could not, however, explain the origin of inertia itself. He tried a thought experiment. He imagined that a bucket of water was the only object in the universe. If so, then how would you measure if it was at rest or rotating? If the sides were curved upward then it must be rotating, but in respect to what? Thus he concluded that there must be some sort of absolute space to measure spatial events against.

A couple of centuries later, Ernst Mach rejected this "absolute space." He agreed with Newton, however, that inertia creates the need for a reference frame of some sort. He postulated that the distant presence of other matter would constitute that reference frame. Yet he came short of defining anything that could actually be proven.

Other physicists in the early twentieth century thought that inertial mass might come from something called "electrostatic self-energy." Any charged particle has a certain amount of electric charge, which is the source of an electric field that carries its electrostatic self-energy. This energy might relate to the inertial mass of the particle via $E=mc^s$. However, when comparing the theoretical mass of the electrostatic particle against that of the particle itself, there was a difference of several orders of magnitude, so that theory failed.

But what if inertia arises from the all-pervasive ZPF?

The ZPF, as we know, should be uniform and the same in all directions. In other words, it is a sea of universe-filling radiation whose emissions rise sharply with increasing frequency. In fact, the energy density increases by the cube of the frequency. At what point does this finally cut off? No one is yet sure.

Let's discuss a side note here, of the origin of the ZPF. We saw in the last chapter that the equations of quantum mechanics demand it. Sometimes it is regarded as a real physical field, and other times as a virtual field that is necessary for solving certain problems. There is a competing explanation for the origin of the ZPF, however. An obscure field of physics known as stochastic electrodynamics (SED), says that the ZPF is as real as any other field of radiation, and a fundamental component of the Universe itself, and not just brought about by a mathematical need to solve some complex problem in quantum mechanics. This fine line of a definition does, however, imply something quite remarkable (at least to a physicist). If you merely add the assumed presence of the ZPF into classical physics, then many phenomena of quantum mechanics can be derived without the need for quantum mechanics' balancing act of esoteric logic. This would make things a lot simpler indeed.

Whichever way the origin of the ZPF goes, the fact is that it exists. But then why—if it is indeed comprised of actual radiation—do people not sense this radiation? Such an immense energy density and no one can detect it? The answer comes in its uniformity. If something is absolutely the same everywhere, whether inside or outside of an object, then there is no way to detect it. If you were to lie perfectly still in a bathtub of body-temperature water, would you know that you were wet, or would you even feel the warmth of the water?

Motion through something is detectable by its wake. For example, a bird flying through the air creates vortices behind it. Or, when you walk on fog, you can see it slowly swirl about you. But, the ZPF is what is termed as Lorentz invariant. No motion through it at a constant velocity is going to disturb it. So no matter how great the energy we sit upon, there is no way to detect that we are sitting. It is only when something is accelerating that the presence of the field can be detected. In other words, when such acceleration distorts the uniformity of the ZPF.

This distortion is, however, very small. It was shown by the same authors of the 1994 article that when an Electro-Magnetically interacting particle is accelerated through the ZPF, a force is exerted on that charge, one that is directly proportional to the acceleration but in the opposite direction. It experiences a force that is proportional to acceleration, just as implied via F=ma. Suddenly "m" is not only mass but a coupling constant. This resistance is the inertia that is an innate property of all matter.

All this suggests that mass does not really exist. Instead, there is an Electro-Magnetic force that acts upon the charge inside of matter to create the effect of inertia. And that statement itself implies that there is no charge *inside* matter. There is *only* charge. Matter is an illusion, created by the interaction of Electro-Magnetic charges with the ZPF. Since even neutral particles such as the neutron are made up of smaller particles with electric charge—quarks, in some theories, or the fact that a neutron can break down into a proton and electron, which carry charge—then this view can be applied to any type of particle around. Hence, the illusive quality of matter.

So, the ZPF explains inertia, but what about gravity? An object's inertial mass is equivalent to its gravitational mass. In fact, Einstein's general theory of relativity is based upon the assumption that inertial and gravitational masses are the same, or at least indistinguishable from one another. So, if the ZPF creates inertia, then it also creates gravity. This was suggested in 1968 by Russian physicist Andrei D. Sakharov and then in 1989 put within the SED framework to yield a nonrelativistic form of Newtonian gravitation.[3]

If a charged particle is subjected to ZPF interactions, then it will fluctuate in response to the random perturbations of the ZPF, which in turn forces all particles in the universe connected through the ZPF to fluctuate as well. Now, all fluctuating electric charges emit E-M radiation, which means that all charges in the universe will emit this secondary E-M field as a result of their interaction with the ZPF. This secondary force is much weaker than the ordinary electrostatic charges, and is always attractive. This sounds like a good definition for the force of gravity to me.

These fluctuations, as it turns out, are relativistic, and the energy associated with them is the energy equivalent of gravitational resting mass. Gravitational force is caused by these fluctuations, so we no longer talk about gravitational rest mass as the source of gravity, but something driven by charge. So back to $E=mc^2$. We now realize that mass is not simply equivalent to energy, but rather mass *is* energy.

Of course, one major objection haunts this theory. That is, if the ZPF is real, and so is its energy, it would be the source of a large enough gravitational field that would have everything squashed like a bug before the universe could get a really good start. The easy solution is to realize that such gravitational force only arises from *perturbations* moving through the field. The ZPF itself is uniform, unperturbed, and hence not a source of gravity, but rather gravity is caused by motion *through* it.

There are still other unanswered questions, of course, such as how to explain certain gravitational effects predicted by general relativity alone and not Newtonian theory. For instance, the slight deflection of light around the gravitational field of a star. Such problems are not deal-breakers, though, merely details that need to be eventually worked out. There is enough worked out right now to draw a reasonable conclusion pertaining to our discussions.

Matter *is* energy. Gravity is the result of objects interacting with the ZPF, like dragging a stick through the surface of a pond. You feel the resistance the water of the pond offers as you move along, just as objects feel the resistance offered by the ZPF. Gravitational force and inertia are direct evidence of the existence of the Zero Point Field. As you feel weight, so does it exist?

Conclusion

We have spent this entire section discussing the strange possibilities brought about by quantum mechanics and the all-pervasive Zero Point Field, the possibilities of manifesting our desires by putting our thoughts into resonance with the energy of the Universe.

Quantum mechanics and biology both point to the one single fact. Thoughts have an energy which is in resonance with the energy of the Universe. And energy is equivalent to mass. Therefore, thoughts are equivalent to mass. Thoughts have power that can manifest into reality. The Zero Point Field is energy and information in one; the ultimate source of potential just waiting for one to tap into it. Time and space do not matter to it, only from our tiny perspectives and how we wish to call forth our desires.

Is this something new brought about by the weird science that is quantum mechanics? Or, have we been told this all before, a very long time ago? It's time to look back into history to see what has been lying beneath our noses all along, as we end this scientific recap to begin our journey into our spiritual history.

Part Two

THE SPIRITUAL

Chapter 8

RELIGIONS OF ABRAHAM

Defining religion might be the best way to start this part. *Religion* "is a collection of cultural systems, belief systems, and worldviews that establishes symbols which relate humanity to spirituality and, sometimes, to moral values."[1]

There are 19 major religious groupings in the world, and from them a total of 10,000 distinct religions, although only about 270 of those have half a million or more followers. In the United States alone, over 2,500 different religious faith entities can be observed. That's a lot of different ways of formulating cultural and belief systems.

In this chapter, we will examine the three so-called religions of Abraham, namely, Judaism, Christianity, and Islam. In the next chapter, we will examine three major religions of insight (or wisdom), namely, Hinduism, Buddhism, and Shinto. Most persons who affiliate or actively participate in a religion will be able to trace their religion back to one or another of these.

Religions of Abraham—Judaism, Christianity, and Islam—have some reference to each other. All three trace their heritage to Abraham, Sarah, and Isaac (Judaism and Christianity) or Abraham, Hagar, and Ismael (Islam). All three believe in one universal God, experienced as personal, who is the creator of the universe and the primary source of values. All three treat their scriptures as revealed truth.

Judaism

Judaism is historically first and traces its history after Abraham (down through his great-grandsons) to Moses, who led slaves out of Egypt into a forty-year exodus, pausing to receive the Ten Commandments from God, and finally settling in the land promised to Abraham. After the twelve tribes settled Canaan, they eventually set up two kingdoms with Saul, David, and Solomon as noteworthy kings. Solomon's Temple in Jerusalem (and the rebuilt version) was the center of a sacrificial system until 70 a.d., when the Temple was again destroyed and Judaism became a home-and-synagogue religion. Many Jews observe the ancient dietary and health practices (keeping kosher) and worship in synagogues.[2]

The stories of Abraham, Moses, and many others indicate how, for Jews, God is experienced in human community in history. Indeed, God had established a covenant with this people and required obedience to it, another way in which God is experienced and through which all of humanity was summoned to acknowledge God's sovereignty and purpose.

Even this chosen community, however, failed to fulfill its promises. So the flow of stories is one of persons being held in oppression, being redeemed, setting up structures (with oppressive elements), and then being held again in bondage. The tradition has constantly searched for additional meaning and insight with collections of comments contained in Midrashim, Targumim, and Talmuds.

Its beliefs and doctrines, however, can be summarized as follows:

— God's sovereignty (rule) is disclosed in nature (through constant renewal) and history (compassion and judgment).

— God as person encounters community and members.

— Communal life and worship needs to exhibit solidarity in all aspects of life; the Shema or confession of faith is, "Hear, O Israel. The Lord our God is one."

Divine love and divine justice—the Creator and Law-giver—are the same.

— God is present, called *Shekhina* ("the Present One"), addressed as "Blessed art Thou ...," and confessed as active in human history, for example, in the Passover meal: "and the Lord brought us forth out of Egypt—not an angel ..." (Seder).

— Upon waking, one gives thanks, as well as each part of returning to the routines of life, ending with a prayer for the establishment of the Kingdom of God, which could be fulfilled today. Prayer and blessings are part of the entire day.

— Keeping kosher in home-centered practices keeps kitchen and dining areas as places of divine-human meeting or dwelling.

— At the center of synagogue life is the reading of Scriptures, which takes place on Sabbath, holy, and festival days as well as on Monday and Thursday mornings and on Sabbath afternoons.

— The Kingdom of God is a rich bank of beliefs variously expressed at different times about how Davidic rule would be restored, how Jews from prior times could return to experience this peace, and how all nations could come to worship God truly.

Christianity

Christianity is the name that outsiders applied to the followers of Jesus. He was a Jew who attended annual Passover (celebration meal to prepare for the Exodus from slavery in Egypt) in Jerusalem. At around age thirty, he declared a public ministry of healing, restoring Israel, and making ready for God's kingdom (or the return of God's Son). This ended in his final Passover with his disciples (Last Supper with followers), arrest, trial, and execution on Good Friday. His followers believe that God raised him from the dead on Easter Sunday, that Jesus' (or the Holy) Spirit was given to the early followers who were sent to baptize new believers with water in God's name.[3]

Jesus is called the Christ because early Jewish followers saw him as the Messiah, whom Judaism had awaited to return and restore Israel. Christians view their Bible as the Old Testament (the Jewish Torah, Prophets, and the Writings) and the New Testament (Gospels, Acts, and Letters). Christians are defined by their belief in the Trinity—God in one substance, but three *personas* (literally "masks"). Most believe in an afterlife in Heaven or on a restored Earth.

Its beliefs and doctrines, can be summarized as follows:

— Christianity as revealed through Jesus is the fulfillment of Jewish revelations and the epitome of all other religions ("the river of truth is one").

— This is because the Logos (the Word or divine reason) embodied in Jesus was there before the world's Creation (see the Nicene Creed).

— Yet, the "wretched fact" is that Jesus was executed by permission of the Roman Empire before he was raised from the dead and ascended into heaven; this fact stands in contrast to any view of a good life.

— So the "Son of Man" or "The Christ" is believed to be returning one day to establish harmony, recompense believers who have suffered, and punish those who have caused suffering.

— Believers are sustained until that day by Jesus' Spirit ("Lo, I am with you always, even to the close of the age").

— The church is the body of Christ composed of those who sacramentally participated in the death and resurrection of Jesus; thus, the dead and still living are part of the same community.

— Jesus charged his followers to make disciples of all nations; this is similar to Siddhartha Gautama (the Buddha) and Muhammad (Islam).

Islam

Islam means "submission" (to the Will of God). One who submits is called a *Muslim*. Islamic doctrine is laid down in the *Qur'an* (literally, "reading" or "recitation;" sometimes spelled, Koran) and the *Sunna* ("customs" or "traditions" of the Prophet). The central doctrine is the absolute unity of God (Allah). At several times in human history, Muslims believe that God has sent prophets, including Hebrew prophets and Jesus, who was a human born of a virgin and only apparently crucified to death. The last of the prophets is Muhammad (570-629 a.d.) who recorded God's divine dictates. The chief practices are confessing faith in Allah and in Muhammad his prophet; praying five times each day facing Mecca; alms giving to the poor; and fasting during the month of Ramadan. Muslims believe in an afterlife.[4]

Its beliefs and doctrines, however, can be summarized as follows:

— God is one and unique; God has no partner, no equal, and formulations such as Christianity's three-in-one are absolutely rejected.

— No intermediaries stand between God and the creation; God created everything by sheer command: Be.

— God is everywhere, but does not inhere in things.

— God is the sole Creator and sustainer of the universe; all of creation bears witness to this unity of Person and action.

— God is just and merciful so that the order of nature is ensured, and this is also God's mercy that the order is personally maintained.

— This understanding of God—in which God's power, justice, and mercy interpenetrate—meshes with the Judeo-Christian tradition from whence it was derived.

— This understanding rejects the pagan Arabian belief in a powerful, but blind and inexorable fate over which persons had no control; instead God is pictured as powerful, but providential and merciful.

— The universe's unity is a reflection of God's unity; the universe has no gaps or dislocations because everything has a clear, definite purpose that fits together, but has clear limits.

— Angels protested the creation of humanity because humans would sow mischief on earth; God created humanity to be noblest of all creation and accept the responsibility for the rest of creation.

— Humanity's purpose is to be in service and obedience to God's will.

— The Qur'an accepts the story of Adam's disobedience, but features God's forgiveness of this act; this is *not* the source of original sin (as for Christians).

— Human nature is frail and faltering; humanity is rebellious and full of pride, especially thinking that each person is or can be self-sufficient. Our chief sin is the pride of self-sufficiency.

— The purpose of sending prophets is to underscore the truth of Divine Unity among us ever prone to forget (or willfully reject) that unity under the promptings of Satan.

— Satan, chief among the angels, fell from Divine favor when Satan refused to honor Adam as God had commanded him to do so; Satan embodies the pride all of humanity faces until the Last Day.

— Yet, even with sealed hearts, sinners can repent and redeem themselves by a genuine conversion to the truth; God is always ready to pardon, which means that all sins are removed and the penitent is restored to a sinless state.

— All prophets are to be acknowledged and honored equally, because all can call humans to repentance.

— Some prophets, however, have been particularly exceptional in steadfastness and patience under trial—Abraham, Noah, Moses, Jesus—and God often saved them with miracles, such as Noah being saved from the Great Flood. Yet, all prophets are human and without any part of divinity.

— On the Last Day, the world comes to an end, the dead are resurrected, and God judges each person according to his or her deeds because sins cannot be fully requited in this life (or goodness rewarded), such judgment is required.

Chapter 9

RELIGIONS OF INSIGHT

In the previous chapter, we delved into three religions that are consciously related to one another. For example, all tell the stories of Abraham, Noah, and Moses, and all three center on God's revelation of divine will and proper living.

In this chapter, we focus on three religions, two of which are connected, namely, Hinduism and Buddhism. Shintoism is the third religion that developed primarily in Japan and is active today. (Historically, another religion developed on the Chinese mainland, Taoism, but it is much less practiced now.)

I call these religions those of insight (or wisdom). Hinduism and Shintoism are amalgamations of the earliest traditions of groups in India and Japan. Buddhism grew out of the Buddha's enlightenment, or insights into reality, suffering, and living.

These could also be termed religions of wisdom. Each offers a knowledge or prudence about how to live well, even in times of desperation.

Hinduism

Hinduism means "civilization of the Hindus" (people of India, Pakistan, Ceylon, Nepal, and Sikkim). Its complexity or diversity comes from its inheritance of many Indo-European belief structures. In principal, Hinduism incorporates all forms of belief and worship, without requiring the elimination or enfranchisement of any. Its core doesn't even depend on the existence or non-existence of God, or on whether there is one or many.[1]

So how do you know if you are speaking with a Hindu? Here are some clues:

— Sole reality (*Brahman*) is an uncreated, eternal, infinite, transcendent, and all-embracing principle that is comprised of both being and non-being.

— *Vishnu* (special manifestation of the preserving function) or *Shiva* (special manifestation of the destructive function) is taken as a favorite god; with *Brahama*, these form the so-called Hindu Trinity.

— Veda is the most ancient collection of writings and is an absolute authority for revealing fundamental and unassailable truth, even though few consult it; Brahmins are a noble class by birth that possesses spiritual supremacy.

— Respect for life (*Ahimsa*) and fellow feeling of all living things means that many followers are vegetarians, and that animals, especially cows, are protected.

— *Karmin* ("previous acts") influences transmigration and rebirth; this entire process is *samsara*.

— *Pravritti* ("acts") has three goals for those who are in the world: (1) *Dharma*: Have righteousness in your life; (2) *Artha*: Have success in your economic and material life; and (3) *Kama*: Achieve gratification of the senses—pleasure, sensual joy, and mental joy.

— *Nivritti* ("knowledge") has one goal for those who have renounced the world and that is *Moksa*, or liberated from *Samsara*.

— *Samsara* is "the wheel of suffering"—the endless cycle of birth, life, death, and rebirth through many lifetimes. The acts of one life, good or bad, determine your karma and the sort of life you will be born into next. This is considered the supreme goal of humanity. The ultimate goal is to escape samsara and achieve enlightenment; to be one with Brahma.

Buddhism

Buddhism traces its beginnings to the life of Gautama Siddhartha, who was born about 563 B.C. in the southern borderland of Nepal. He soon realized the futility of social life because philosophical discussions often prevent right living. The shadow of death follows all living creatures. Stories suggest that after encounters with a sick man, an old man, a dead man, and a serene mendicant ascetic, Gautama decided to abandon his home, wife, and son. Instead he associated with the most famous spiritual masters of his time. Effective meditation, he learned, requires a healthy body, and leads to correct knowledge about the nature of all things, both in their appearance and disappearance. So, under a pipal tree in Bodh Gaya, he achieved enlightenment (*bodhi*) and thus became the (or a) Buddha ("enlightened one").[2]

— The Hindu gods Indra and Brahma came down from the heavens and begged Gautama to reveal this liberating doctrine to all, which he did until his death.

— There is no essential or ultimate reality in things, no soul, nothing within us that is metaphysically real.

— We are caught in a cycle of births and deaths because un-extinguished good deeds mean a projection toward a new existence.

— From this, the Buddha taught the Four Noble Truths: (1) Misery is our life; (2) Misery originates in us because of our craving for pleasures; (3) This craving can be extinguished; and (4) The Path of Enlightenment is the means to achieve *Nirvana*, "a state of eternal bliss" in which you can want for nothing and have everything you need.

The Eightfold Path of Enlightenment is a guideline that is often divided into three groups. By following these guides, one can achieve

Nirvana, which is an afterlife of sorts, one with many of the promises implied in a heavenly state, but without the deities involved.

This Eightfold Path is summed up below, divided into its three groupings.

— *Panna* ("discernment or wisdom" has two aspects: *Samma ditthi* ("right understanding of the Four Noble Truths") and *Samma sankappa* ("right thinking;" following the right path in life).

— *Sila* ("virtue, morality") has three aspects: *Samma vaca* ("right speech;" no lying, criticism, condemning, gossip, or harsh language); *Samma kammanta* ("right conduct by following the Five Precepts"); and *Samma ajiva* ("right livelihood;" support yourself without harming others).

— *Samadhi* ("concentration, meditation") has three aspects: *Samma vayama* ("right effort; promote good thoughts; conquer evil thoughts); *Samma sati* ("right mindfulness;" become aware of your body, mind, and feelings; and *Samma Samadhi* ("right concentration;" meditate to achieve a higher state of consciousness).

It is believed that by following these practices one will, in some lifetime, be able to fully release their attachment to desire and the self, and thence attain Nirvana. Along the way, the focus of the mind through meditation can often lead one into experiencing what might be known of as miracles. In Buddhism, you do not pray for everyday needs, but rather a greater insight into the world, and for a perfect state of being in the afterlife.

Shintoism

Shinto, an ancient religion in Japan, means "the way of *kami* (or 'divine powers')." It began as a mixture of fertility cults, nature and hero worship, shamanism, and the worship of multiple deities. It is not as organized or centralized as other religions, and does not have its own moral code. Rather, the code of Confucianism or Buddhism is inserted. The Kami are the gods and spirits of the world, with rituals involving prayers and offerings to the Kami to gain their favor in times of trouble or need. If there is something in your life that you need to improve, then either prayer to the appropriate Kami in order to gain their favor is one action, or be respectful of nature and the world. In this view, all living things are children of the Kami and are thus deeply interconnected.[3]

Shinto itself tells the stories of the spirits and deities, or "Kami," that created the world and all within it. Most of Shinto dealt with its creation mythology and how to honor the Kami. Ancestors were deeply revered and worshipped, and all life and nature was considered sacred since it all sprang from the mother goddess, Amaterasu Omikami. Beyond that, Shinto did not have its own inherent moral code. It was not until the absorption of Buddhism that Shinto gained a morality. The concepts in Buddhism were adapted to the needs of Shinto to make it the religion that it is today.

There are four "affirmations" in Shinto:

— Tradition and the family: The family is the main device by which traditions are preserved; birth and marriage comprise the majority of their celebrations.

— Love of nature: Nature is sacred; natural objects are worshipped as sacred spirits.

— Physical cleanliness: "Cleanliness is next to godliness" has particular importance with them.

— *Matsuri*: The worship and honor given to the Kami and ancestral spirits.

Beliefs in the mysterious power of the kami are at the center of Shinto. The nature of kami cannot adequately be put into words because kami transcends human faculties of understanding, yet, truly devoted followers can understand the kami through faith, and these kami have a polytheistic character (many gods or divinities). Each kami has a divine personality, and truthful prayers can elicit a response from the kami, such as *makoto*, which guides the faithful to live in accord with it. The kami cooperate with one another, and when one lives in accord with a kami, all the others assist in protecting and otherwise assisting the believer.

Believers develop the attitude of *magokoro* ("true heart and bright, pure mind") while doing their best in their relations with others. This leads to personal moral virtues, such as loyalty and faithfulness. This is because each person is kami's child, meaning each has a sacred nature. Purification in both mind and body is necessary for the communion of kami, as well as to receive the kami's blessing.

Each person in unity with the kami deserves the respect of others. This is not because of human original sinfulness—an unknown concept to the Shinto—but because each person is part of a long chain of ancestors behind, as well as a long chain of descendants looking forward. There is no last day or judgment. History develops eternally, just as the sun rises without end, thus the most important time is the present, right now.

Ethic of Reciprocity

Jesus in his Sermon on the Mount (as written in the gospel Matthew) or Sermon on the Plain (as in Luke) charges his followers, "Do unto others as you would have them do unto you." A Targum in Judaism says the same, and a law in Leviticus states the negative. Islam has its own version. Perhaps this connection should not be surprising, given that these three religions all have a common ancestral origin for what is known more generally as the "Ethic of Reciprocity."[4]

What might be surprising, however, is just how many of the world's other religions have this same or similar rule. In other words, religions with completely different origins and no ancient intermixing offer their followers a similar command or insight. Here is a quick recap of others' versions of this same rule or ethic.

Bahá'í Faith:"Ascribe not to any soul that which thou wouldst not have ascribed to thee, and say not that which thou doest not.""Blessed is he who prefers his brother before himself." *Baha'u'llah*

"And if thine eyes be turned toward justice, choose thou for thy neighbor that which thou choosest for thyself." *Epistle to the Son of the Wolf.*

Brahmanism:	**"This is the sum of Dharma: Do naught unto others which would cause you pain if done to you".** *Mahabharata, 5:1517*
Buddhism:	**"Treat not others in ways that you yourself would find hurtful."** *Buddha.*
	"Hurt not others in ways that you yourself would find hurtful." *Udana-Varga 5:18*
Christianity:	**"Therefore all things whatsoever ye would that men should do to you, do ye even so to them: for this is the law and the prophets."** *Matthew 7:12* **(King James Version.)**
	"And as ye would that men should do to you, do ye also to them likewise." *Luke 6:31* **(KJV)**
Confucianism:	**"Do not do to others what you do not want them to do to you"** *Analects 15:23*
	"Tse-kung asked, 'Is there one word that can serve as a principle of conduct for life?' Confucius replied, 'It is the word 'shu' —-reciprocity. Do not impose on others what you yourself do not desire.'" *Doctrine of the Mean 13.3*
Ancient Egyptian:	**"Do for one who may do for you, that you may cause him thus to do."** *The Tale of the Eloquent Peasant, 109 —110* **Translated by R.B. Parkinson (Original circa 1800 B.C.)**

Hinduism:	"This is the sum of duty: do not do to others what would cause pain if done to you." *Mahabharata 5:1517*
Islam:	"None of you truly believes until he wishes for his brother what he wishes for himself." *Number 13 of Imam 'Al-Nawawi's Forty Hadiths'* (One of 43 sayings of the Prophet Muhammad)
Janism:	"Therefore, neither does he cause violence to others nor does he make others do so." *Acarangasutra 5.101-2*
	"In happiness and suffering, in joy and grief, we should regard all creatures as we regard our own self." *Lord Mahavira, 24th Tirthankara*
	"A man should wander about treating all creatures as he himself would be treated." *Sutrakritanga 1.11.33*
Judaism:	"... thou shalt love thy neighbor as thyself." *Leviticus* **19:18**
	"What is hateful to you, do not to your fellow man. This is the law: all the rest is commentary." *Talmud, Shabbat 31a*
	"And what you hate, do not do to any one." *Book of Tobit 4:15*

Conclusion

These religions seem to have more than a few key concepts in common, some of which I want to lift up at the close of this chapter:

— They mostly worship a divine spirit or spirits that are (or are connected with) the Universe as a whole, although Buddhism may be the exception in that the one with enlightenment becomes a god.

— They each have a code of proper morale conduct; even Shintoism, which borrows its code from either Buddhism or Confucianism, does in practice have one.

— They all have a tradition of prayer or meditation to curry divine favor or self-insight.

— They all have a way, usually through prayer, to affect each believer's ultimate life's outcome, whether addressing a God that created the Universe, or the Universe itself, with expectation of a reward or better outcome next go-around.

Prayer and meditation are sending out your thoughts into the Universe to change your reality. Hmm. Sounds as though enough similarities exist here to warrant further investigation. Let us delve, then, into the details of these religions a bit further as we continue our investigation.

Chapter 10

MIRACLES

Miracles are a common cornerstone in many religions. But, what exactly is a miracle, and how and why do they occur? Are they manifestations of the Zero Point Field, or did God really come down and flex some power? What we do know is that, no matter the religion or part of the world where it happens, there is some commonality to all miracles.[1]

In all cases, prayer is a significant player. Prayer and the presence of a strong need felt by all present and involved. Ever heard of a miracle where the people involved weren't asking for it? Neither have I. But, before we go any further, let us cite some examples, and not just from the Christian Bible but from several diverse sources. If miracles are indeed thoughts being manifested through the Zero Point Field, then they should occur no matter the religion, nationality, or area of the world.

The Parting of the Red Sea

This is possibly the most famous miracle of them all, so we'll start out with this one. According to the Hebrew Bible, Moses requested that Pharaoh let the Hebrews (who were now slaves) to go out from Egypt. When Pharaoh denied this request, Moses foretold of ten plagues that would be visited on the Egyptians, the final one being the death of the first born (including livestock) in each household that did not sprinkle blood from a lamb on the door frame with a hyssop branch.[2]

When the bloody water, frogs, and the other plagues didn't convince the Pharaoh to free the Israelites (Hebrews), Moses told them to cook light that evening, for example, make bread without any leaven, keep their cloaks at the ready, and be prepared to flee. As the cries of grief went up in Egypt, Moses led his people out of Egyptian slavery to march toward the Promised Land. When Pharaoh saw this, he ordered his officers to take more than 600 chariots to stop the emigration.

Just as the army was closing in, the Israelites could no longer move ahead; they were stopped by the Red Sea. Behind them were Pharaoh's soldiers, ready to slaughter the Israelites in retaliation for the grief they had caused. The Israelites cried out to Moses, "Were their not enough graves in Egypt that you have brought us here to die in the wilderness?"

Then God commanded Moses to lift his walking stick; a ferocious wind came, and the Israelites walked across the sea on dry land. The angel who had been leading the escape moved to the rear and the pillar of cloud (which was a pillar of flame at night) also moved between the people and the army to block the soldiers from getting to them. When the Israelites had finished their crossing, and after Pharaoh and his officers entered the dry path, the winds ceased and waters closed, drowning the approaching army.

This story piles on the miracles until it's hard to count them. Can some scientific explanation be given? Perhaps. Does this make these miracles any less? For example, observations have been made about how the Red Sea can draw back from time to time given the right circumstances, including its low depth in some spots at some times during the year. Add in a really stiff breeze to push back the remaining water, and you could have a parting across it wide enough for some fleeing ex-slaves to run through. It's even possible for it to stay that way long enough for the good guys to get through, and also theoretically

Not true

possible for the waters to return just in time to drown the Pharaoh's troops as a bonus.

These are a lot of small probabilities, though. The Red Sea reaches its low just after the Israelites get there along with that stiff breeze, and lasts long enough and cuts off right when it's needed, while the pillar of cloud is delaying the troops. All of these assumptions are technically possible, but the probability of all these conditions coming together at the same time would be extremely miniscule. That's why it's called a miracle, because it *had* to be the Hand of God.

Or did it? You have a few thousand people hoping for a miracle, crying out for deliverance or being led in prayer by Moses, whose faith that something would happen was unshakable. That's the faith of a few thousand people all praying and hoping for the same thing, and all focused intently on the object of escape. Suddenly, our probability is influenced by this collective focus, and we get a highly improbable event manifesting itself. Was this a miracle, or the will of the people?

The Ice Bridge Miracle at Cap de la Madeleine

Quebec, Canada, has a shrine called the Shrine of the Cap, or Cap de la Madeleine, which is a former town at the confluence of the Saint-Maurice River and the St. Lawrence River. The winter of 1878-79 was so mild that ice did not form on the river. Father Luc Desilets needed to get some stone building blocks across the river to build the shrine with them. Unfortunately, without a bridge of ice on the river, the task seemed impossible. Yet, Father Desilets asked the people to pray for a bridge of ice to form on the river so they could use it to cross. Everyone began praying, including the young associate pastor, Father Duquay, who prayed the rosary at a side chapel in front of the altar at the Feet of Our Lady of the Cap. The people and priests prayed from November to March, when a high wind began to break up the ice blocking the mouth of the adjoining river upstream, and the chunks floated down to the Cap. They chunks covered the river several hundred feet from the church.[3]

On the Feast of Saint Patrick's, Father Duquay told the parishioners there would be a high mass to pray for a bridge of ice to form. He then took some men to survey the river. A thin layer of ice had formed between the floating blocks of ice, but too thin to hold any weight. So, they persisted until they found a stretch of stable ice wide enough to carry carts laden with stones. They then began pouring more water over that stretch of ice so it would freeze and thicken, until in two days time it had thickened to six inches. On March nineteenth, enough snow had fallen the previous night to block all but one way across the ice; the same path they had spotted before. A stable bridge of ice had formed, and they were able to pass 175 stone-laden sleighs across the frozen river.

The Bridge was given the name the Bridge of the Rosary. Since then an actual stone bridge has been built in its place. A miracle had been asked for, not just a vague "please save us" miracle, but a specific one. People of faith prayed and their need was answered. A miracle sent from God, and backed by the collective prayers of an entire congregation.

The Anistasis

Some years ago, around 1996, a religious group called "Youth with a Mission" bought a ship, called the *Anistasis* ("resurrection" in Greek), to spread the message of Jesus in word and deed. They equipped the ship for use as a hospital, including dental surgery, and loaded it with supplies needed for building houses, schools, and clinics in developing countries. Over the years, the ship and its volunteer crew have given much practical help in many Third World countries.[4]

They were able to buy the ship, but because of a shortage of both personnel and finances, the ship lay unused in a Greek harbor for three years, so the project's director suggested that he and the entire crew fast for 40 days, following the example set by Jesus to show that they were serious in their intentions. That was 40 days of fasting, praying, and faith.

Toward the end of the 40 days of fasting, a series of miracles occurred. The first happened as a Moroccan crew member was walking along the beach and twelve fish leapt out of the water to his feet. Later a large fish sprang out of the sea at the feet of the chief engineer and his family as they walked by the water's edge. On day 38 of the fast, an American girl who was a member of the volunteer crew was sitting on the beach when two-hundred-and-ten fish landed near her. The following day, while the crew was praying for Greece and the needs of the world, one of the crew members shouted, "The fish are coming!" Everyone rushed outside. This time 8,301 fish had jumped out of the sea and onto the beach. Despite efforts to return the fish to the sea, they kept leaping out again and landing at the feet of the crew. Eventually the fish were collected, cleaned, and salted. For the next six weeks the crew ate fish at least once a week.

The "miracle of the fish" so encouraged the crew that the ship was soon able to sail, and shortly thereafter experienced another miracle: donations totaling $600,000 came in to support their project.

Once again, people prayed, and miracles happened that fulfilled their needs, not in some historically distant time, but in modern times. Probably within your lifetime. There could well be solid scientific explanations for why the fish wanted to leave the water so badly, but the miracle part would be in the timing of it. Just like for Moses, the coincidences and improbabilities occurred just when they were needed.

The Miami Man who Was Prayed Back to Life

In 2007, Dr. Chauncay Crandall tells of a 53 year-old man in Miami Florida, who came to the emergency room with a massive heart attack. The patient's heart had stopped, and after he received treatments for 40 minutes, he was declared dead. The nurse was preparing the body so that it could be taken to the morgue when, Dr. Crandall said, the

Holy Spirit told him to pray for the man. He did, praying out loud for the man to be brought back to life. A couple of minutes later, the man's heart started beating again, and shortly thereafter he started moving his fingers and mumbling.[4]

When the man had recovered, he told of how he had thought himself in a dark room, no light, and no one around, and no one caring. He felt just as if strangers would have thrown him there. Then he was returned.

The brain continues to function for a few minutes after the heart stops bringing fresh oxygen-filled blood, and after death has been declared, so that would explain the man's memory of when he was "dead." Even though medical science had declared him dead, a small part of him was still lingering. Yet, something had to bring him back and restart his heart. The doctor prayed and minutes later the man was returned. This case was witnessed by the nurse and documented.

One might still view the timing of this as a coincidence. This was the second time it had happened with this doctor, however. On a previous case, it was a similar situation; a patient had failed to survive a heart attack, died on the operating table, and minutes after the doctor began praying for him out loud. The patient revived to the surprise of the attending nurse.

The doctor is a religious man, and believes it was the power of his faith in God and prayer that performed the miracle. Faith—and the power of focused thought manifesting?

A Nun's Parkinson's Cure

This story also broke in 2007 when a 45 year old French Nun in Lyon was cured of Parkinson's disease. She had been diagnosed in 2001. By 2005, she was too weak to even watch Pope John Paul II on television as he gave his final Easter blessing from the Vatican. In June 2005, the pope had passed away from Parkinson's himself.

The nun's mother superior suggested she pray to the pope. So, she wrote down her prayer with great difficulty and nearly illegibly. Now, Parkinson's disease is not something from which you get cured overnight or currently cured of at all. The next morning, however, the nun woke up and jumped right out of bed, and her body was no longer rigid. Over the next three or four days, her symptoms each disappeared until a doctor confirmed that her Parkinson's disease was in full remission. She attributes it as a miracle from the spirit of Pope John Paul II.

Was it a miracle brought about by a dead pope or by the faith the nun had in that pope? Faith is what is needed for such miracles, but it need not always be faith in oneself. The idea here is that there is either faith in a symbol, faith in another or just faith in *something*. Such faith empowers the individual with focus enough to achieve the miraculous as this case demonstrates.

Levitation

The miracle of levitation is not specific to Indian holy men. A Catholic monk from the 1600s, St. Joseph of Copetino, was seen to levitate while in a deep trance, although he floated often in an uncontrolled manner. His ability to stay afloat for several minutes was witnessed by the Duke of Brunswick, the High Admiral of Castile, and Pope Urban VIII.[5]

Other known levitators are Saint Francis of Paula, Gemma Galgani (a Passionist nun), Saint Benedict, Saint Philip of Neri, Saint Teresa of Avila, and Simon Magnus. In all cases, they were said to perform the feat only while in a state of deeply religious prayer and floated up to a couple of feet above the ground.[6]

In the case of Simon Magus, though, he was judged evil and excommunicated. Was this perhaps because he was able to do it without being deeply religious? Maybe he had another way of focusing other than prayer, and that brought judgment against him as evil in the mindset of the times. Whatever the reason, he was able to levitate just as well as the saints.

Jack Webber, a Welshman, lived from 1907 to 1940. He was a well-known medium who, while in a deep trance, could levitate small tables and other objects. Photographs of such levitations exist. After his death, however, skeptics have decried his tricks as being hoaxes; however, no evidence of fraud was ever found. Whether he was legitimate and merely copied by later false mediums, or was a false medium himself, he again leaves open the possibility that one does not have to be holy to levitate. Webber performed his acts while in a deep meditation or trance, much in the manner of the more religious examples.

During the final revision period of writing this book, I began a relationship with a young woman whose mother is a yoga teacher. The woman attended classes with her mother as her instructor. Over a period of a few years of practice, the woman was able to levitate. I personally witnessed this act and remain fully convinced of its authenticity.

Healing Miracles

Claims for miracles of healing span all religions and times, ranging from ancient history to the present day. The healing miracles of Jesus are documented well enough in the Bible, yet, down through the ages various saints are attributed with having healed by touch. Holy men in India have also been known to have miraculous healing powers.[7]

Whether from Judaism, Christianity, or Islam, or whether the person be lay or clergy—these all have one thing in common: All such miracles were done while someone was in a state of prayer, devotion, trance, or meditation. The only ones seen apparently to perform such healing or other types of miracles without benefit of some sort of mental focus, were those who were later revealed to be guilty of fraud.

A quick search on the Internet will return hundreds of pages where people list their own personal stories of unexplained miraculous healings, including a few videos. To be clear, by *miracle* I mean something beyond the range of normal medical healing. Healing a broken arm within minutes, for instance, is a miracle; doing so over a period of weeks is not. Just like for the nun with Parkinson's disease who was cured overnight, such miracles abound if you look for them.

Summary

So miracles exist, all sourced from a spiritual foundation, be it religious or meditative in nature. In all cases it involves prayer or deep meditation, so then we must ask such questions as:

— Is there a similarity between prayer and meditation?

— What happens while in such a state?

— How prayer or meditation related to "having faith?"

We shall examine such questions in the next chapter.

Chapter 11

MEDITATION, PRAYER, AND FAITH

What difference, if any, stands between meditation and prayer? In observing how persons use these terms, I have concluded the following: *Meditation* often uses practices or exercises for concentrating upon objects of devotion. Such practices attempt either to restrict awareness by focusing attention on, a wise saying or sound, or to enhance awareness by becoming fully contemplative of one's external environment. Some Eastern religions also speak of a third or middle way: focusing on a mental state emptied of all thoughts or perceptions.

Prayer, in contrast, is a deeply spiritual practice whose purpose is to contact or approach God (by whichever name you use), and ask for a change in your life, by purging or cleansing your soul or transforming of your current life and future afterlife. Prayer's purpose is to commune with the deity and includes unconscious or nonverbal expressions at its deepest.

Sounds like there might be a bit of overlap there. How does faith relate to these two practices? *Faith* as used in Jewish, Christian, and Muslim contexts often refers to obedient assent to revealed truth. Used in this way, faith separates prayer from meditation in that the religions of Abraham all practice prayer with less attention paid to meditation.

Yet, *faith* can also be understood as bedrock trust and loyalty that gives you a sense of self in relationships. Used in this way, faith unites prayer and meditation, which are ways of centering self with divinity. Persons who feel mired in feelings of separation can experience God's grace as uplifting and integrating.

Meditation

The basics of meditation are to sit quietly and not think. There are several ways of doing this, but they all boil down to getting away from the noise and distraction of the world, quieting the mind of all concern for the daily life, and only when the mind is like a still pond let it run loose to focus on that which is desired. There are several methods and definitions of meditation, which may be why some people have a hard time understanding exactly what it is.

Roger Walsh and Shauna L. Shapiro define meditation, in an article in the 2006 issue of *American Psychologist*, as "a family of self-regulation practices that focus on training attention and awareness in order to bring mental processes under greater voluntary control and thereby foster general mental well-being and development and/or specific capacities such as calm, clarity, and concentration."

B. Rael Cahn and John Polich, in a 2006 article in *Psychology Bulletin*, define meditation as "practices that self-regulate the body and mind, thereby affecting mental events by engaging a specific attentional set. Regulation of attention is the central commonality across the many divergent methods."

In contrast, Jevning, R. K. Wallace and M. Beidebach, in a 1992 article of *Neuroscience & Biobehavioral Reviews*, says, "We define meditation ... as a stylized mental technique ... repetitively practiced for the purpose of attaining a subjective experience that is frequently described as very restful, silent, and of heightened alertness, often characterized as blissful."

There are enough differences just in these three definitions to cause a little bit of confusion. Moreover, some say that meditation can be deeply spiritual or religious, while others say that it is restful and energizing. So, just what is the common thread?

Some forms of meditation have you sit in a certain posture, close your eyes, and blank out your mind. Others involve keeping your eyes open, but keeping them focused on an object, such as a flickering flame or small object. In some practices, you need to visualize something, and in many forms there is a certain breathing technique, which must accompany the meditation. Many practices have you focus on a word or phrase, called a mantra, which is repeated constantly throughout the meditation. In some religious variations, such as in Islam, this word or phrase can be taken from a holy scripture. There are literally thousands of specific styles and methods for meditating, but they all amount to the same goal: quiet the mind.

The way one sits, in whichever style, is more to achieve a compromise between comfort and alertness; you aren't trying to go to sleep, after all. Beyond that, the breathing, visualizations, and everything else, are there to get your mind off the outside world and focused on your own inside world, and to bring the mind into a single strict focus instead of the multitasking mayhem it usually is. Just getting this far, bringing the mind to a point of total focus, is difficult enough, and its accomplishment just marks the beginning.

The goal of meditation is not only to achieve that focus but also to do something with it. Some ancient practices use this point to gain a more spiritual state, and to connect with the Universe (be it Brahma, God, or whatever). Others use it to develop mental clarity, clearer thinking, increased visual perception, or press human capability to miraculous levels. The less spiritual simply use it as stress relief while some meditate on a specific desire or outcome to gain enlightenment into its solving, or to connect with the universe for a solution. In all cases, this focus achieved through meditation allows one to touch something deep within himself, which is something often described as spiritual in nature. This something can bring joy, enlightenment, a deep understanding within yourself, or even affect a change within yourself and the world around you. For those who have achieved this ultimate goal of meditation, it has been likened to touching the Infinite.

This sounds like a perfect definition of God and a good lead-in to the next section.

Prayer

When you pray, what is it that you are doing? Sitting or kneeling quietly, your mind focused only on your devotion to god, and either quietly reciting your chosen prayer or sending up your specific needs. The more deeply in prayer you are, the less aware of the outside world you become. There are monks and priests who pray for hours, and spend that entire time focused on their one prayer and on the single thought of God. They recite their prayers, often the same one over and over.

During my time living amongst Tibetan Monks at the Lama temple in Beijing, China, I interviewed a young monk and asked him how much time he spent in a meditative state. He said he did not know. I cross examined him for several minutes and could not get a straight answer. In between each question his attention went back to his mala beads. He was meditating all the time he that he was not actively answering questions. The beads became his bridge to focusing on his faith in the Buddha. He was training his brain to go into Faith Wave.

This sounds sort of like a mantra in meditation. Think about it. When you say the Rosary, what are you doing? Repeating a single prayer over and again. That's exactly like a mantra. Jewish mystics use a series of *kavanot* (prayers) in order to steer prayers to God. Muslims pray Salah five times each day.

What else might prayer have in common with meditation? Well, you're sitting quietly, tuning out the outside world and your normal concerns to focus on the praying. You are trying to bring the mind to a focus to connect with God. If you are praying on a specific matter, then you are focused on that one single desire and asking God for insight or a solution for your problem. Some people focus on an image of Christ or God or their prayer rug when praying, or on a small object, such as a cross or Jewish prayer beads. Many religious men, when praying deeply and long enough, have reported the sensation of touching God, feeling God's presence within them.

Substitute "Infinite" for "God" and it sounds exactly like meditation. In both cases you tune out everything around you, focus on one thing, and try to touch something far greater than yourself. If you have a problem you need solved, you pray for a solution or meditate on the outcome. Meditation uses breathing, mantras, focus on something such as a flame or small object, or visualization to achieve the proper focus; prayer uses a mantra of prayers, the visualization of religious symbols, or focus on an object of religious significance. If God is Infinite, then what is the difference?

The point is prayer is another form of meditation; they are exactly the same. It doesn't make a difference whether one focuses on a prayer or mantra, or on a flickering flame or a cross. You are trying to achieve the same state of spirituality in either case, so it's just the names that change. And before we get caught up in the old, "Yes, but he's not praying to God, so he's a heathen and evil", thing, let us hark back to our definitions of religion. Allah, Brahma, or the Infinite, are all just different names for the same thing based on what arbitrary definition we give Him, we simply see Him from different angles.

simply not True

There are even many major religions that have their own meditation practices worked in with their prayer rituals. Judaism has Kabbalah, which is a meditative study taught to those over the age of forty. Meditation has always been at the core of Judaism. Hinduism uses meditation and yoga as a part of their religious practices. Muslim prayer involves meditating on God. Even Christianity acknowledges a form of meditation upon God that falls a bit deeper than vocal prayer.

So, prayer and meditation are both the same process; a means of touching our spirit to the greater spirit of the Infinite. But, where does Faith come in?

Faith

Faith, in a religious context, means that you accept as genuine God's revealed truth (the religions of Abraham; the Eight-fold Path of Enlightenment). Prayer in this religious sense means you trust in God, that you are absolutely dependent upon God to provide for you, and that God will offer a solution to your problems. You are completely certain of it and so you ask through prayer.

How about faith in a meditative sense? You still need it. After all, if you don't believe that the Infinite will provide your answers, if you don't believe that you can connect with a greater realm and gain enlightenment, then why are you wasting all that time meditating? Meditation has its own component of faith, just as praying does. You focus on one thought, one desire, and have faith that a solution will come to you. Be it in prayer or meditation, faith is needed for both.

So what is a good definition of Faith? It means having certain expectation of a desired result. No distractions in the mind to point a part of your attention to other undesirable outcomes, and no inner voice nagging you about all the reasons why it can't be achieved. Faith is focus and clarity of mind.

Harking back to *The Point of Power*, we can already see some similarities. Remember in that first book, we said that when you focus on a desired outcome, and set it loose into the universe, you need to believe in it completely for it to work, or else you are sending the universe mixed signals. You need to have faith.

So, faith is a key component of prayer or meditation, which are together one and the same. Knowing this, we can delve a bit into what science has been discovering about meditation and apply it to prayer as well.

The Science of Meditation

The brain operates on a variety of frequencies, depending on the current activity involved. Beta is the name for waves in the range of 13 to 40 hertz, and humans generate them when they are active and busy, or concentrating on something. Alpha has a range of 7 to 13 hertz, and occurs while one is relaxed but awake. Delta has a frequency range of less than 4 hertz, and only happens while one is in a deep dreamless sleep. Theta waves have a range of 4 to 7 hertz and occur when one is dreaming, hypnotized, or in deep meditation.

It is this last which is of interest to our subject. Theta brain waves have a high presence in children, extroverts, artists, and people who know how to meditate effectively. Theta waves can be a source of creativity, intuition, more emotional sensitivity, and the lowering of stress and anxiety. Theta waves can also provide a stronger connection with your subconscious, even to allowing you to reprogram it, improve your learning ability, focus your concentration, and improve your body's healing and immune system. So, having a higher presence of Theta waves in your brain has certain benefits, and meditation can help you get there.

Studies done by Yale, Harvard, and Massachusetts General Hospital have all shown that meditation increases gray matter in the brain and slows down any aging-related deterioration. One experiment compared twenty individuals with intensive Buddhist meditation training versus fifteen who did not meditate. Brain scans showed that the meditators have an increased thickness of gray matter in the parts of the brain that are responsible for attention and processing sensory input. Such an increase is proportional to the amount of meditation. Research from Harvard Medical School has also found that during meditation there is a decrease in respiration and heart rate and an increase in blood oxygen saturation levels.

Another study examined a group of colleges' students who were asked to use a form of meditation called "integrative body-mind training."

The study concluded that meditating may "improve the integrity and efficiency of certain connections in the brain" through an increase in their number and robustness. Subsequent brain scans showed strong white matter changes in the anterior cingulate cortex.

Dr. James Austin, a neurophysiologist at the University of Colorado, reported in his book, *Zen and the Brain* (Austin, 1999) that Zen Meditation rewires the brain's circuitry. This has been confirmed using functional MRI imaging.

Gamma waves are another frequency of brain waves, usually in the 25 to 100 hertz range, and are thought to be related to meditation and a higher sense of consciousness. They are intermittent in most people and appear to be localized to select regions of the brain; those associated with long-term meditation. There is some thought that Gamma waves may be related to the sense of unity persons in deep mediation can achieve, though not all agree that this occurs. It may be that this is the frequency range needed to access the Infinite; our Faith Wave.

Whichever the result about Gamma waves, Theta waves are the known connection with meditation, and various techniques exist to help someone try and increase his Theta waves, as this often leads to an overall increase in mental capacity, creativity, and the ability to handle stress.

When in the Theta state, the brain produces several beneficial hormones and neuropeptides, such as serotonin, endorphins, and melatonin that reduce stress, increase relaxation and the ability to learn. Whenever your brainwaves enter into the Theta state, endorphins are made that improve overall thinking ability, improving memory and learning. There is even some research suggesting that endorphins can reverse amnesia to some degree. Serotonin causes one to relax, can relieve pain, and possibly relieve depression. The last neuropeptide, Melatonin, gives you better sleep and slows down the aging process; important since Melatonin is known to decrease with age if you don't keep it up with enough sleep or regular meditation.

For the many cycles of frequencies that the brain goes through in the course of a day, each with its own purpose, Theta waves are best for achieving the benefits associated with meditation. Meditation allows one to alter the operating frequency of the brain, but often takes a lot of practice. One solution was the discovery that sound waves can alter and control the brain's frequencies, but with the realization that such ranges are below the 20 Hz range. This solution was thought impossible since that is below most people's hearing. Binaural Beats, though, came as one solution. Put on a pair of headphones and, through each ear, play a sound that differs in frequency from the other by the amount you would like to induce; in this case, say about 7. The brain will compensate for the difference by producing a tone that will be exactly the difference between the two. So, if you play a 250Hz tone in one ear and a 257Hz tone in the other, your brain will hear a 7Hz tone within itself.

So Binaural Beats are one way to shortcut the process of increasing your Theta waves, but whichever the method, the point is that there is a physical causality that has been measured by science. Meditation increases Theta waves, which have a measurable effect on the body and brain. Meditation also affects Gamma Waves, which may be responsible for that sense of unity with the Infinite, that feeling of being one with God.

Some forms of meditation are aimed at training one's attention for the sake of provoking insight. A wider attention span makes it easier to be aware of a situation, to be objective in emotional and moral situations, and easier to achieve what one might term as a flow state. A *flow* is a state of easy creativity that might be recognized by artists and writers or anyone who has ever been "in the zone." We reference the work of Mihaly Csikszentmihalyi pertaining to Flow (University of Chicago) in some detail in *The Point of Power* book.[2]

Tibetan monk Rinpoche has allowed himself to be subjected to various scientific tests over the years, so that people can better understand the nature and effects of meditation. This included a series of MRI tests at Wisconsin University. It was determined that the brain changes significantly during meditation. Rinpoche's Gamma synchronocity—a measure of how well groups of neurons can work together —was at a height never before measured. Moreover, though it had increased through meditation, it remained high even *after* meditation had ceased. This demonstrates that the brain is physically altered by meditation, and that its plasticity does not disappear after childhood. It continues to develop throughout your entire life.

The point here is that science has confirmed physical benefits and changes brought about by meditation; meditation and prayer being one and the same, so the same could then be said of anyone in a deep state of prayer as well. What can be said about one can now be said about the other. Meditation and prayer have measurable benefits, and both are held in place by faith. We also have the science to show that something physical is happening.

So let us take the next step. How can we use meditation, or prayer, to achieve miracles? Is there a science behind this, or at least a starting point? Considering how long both have been around, one would think a methodology in this has been established. So, let us next examine how it is said that prayer and mediation can be used to manifest our miracles and affect changes in our lives. Maybe we'll find this has something in common with our main theme after all.

Chapter 12

MEDITATING ON MIRACLES

When you need something to happen or change in your life, what do you do? Do you sit down and pray for it? Should this need arise while you are meditating, do you mediate on the subject until a solution presents itself? Do you prefer one over the other? For either approach, what exactly is the accepted process by which you pray or meditate on that miracle that you need?

Now, let's up the ante. What if you need a miracle and not just the more generic "give me good fortune" or "I need the rent" type prayers. What if this miracle was more biblical-proportion, life-changing stuff? I have seen results from miracles that have happened because someone prayed for them. How about you? So how exactly are you supposed to pray or meditate? What difference, if any, is there between the two approaches?

Details will vary depending on who you ask or from which tradition it comes, but there are enough commonalities to draw up a good outline.

How to Meditate on Miracles

Whether you believe in Brahma, God, or simply some universal higher power, there are several things upon which the religious traditions behind these all seem to agree. This higher power is everywhere and everything; everything in this and every other world is a part of it, including you and me. Everyone has potential access to this power, yet only believers have true access. If you don't believe that you can access this higher self that you have, then you shut off the channel immediately. So, the first and most significant component here is belief; faith in yourself that you can access this power. You need open-mindedness and a confidence that you can do this, and that you can create miracles the same as Moses or any of the other prophets.

You might say, "Wait. I am not Moses or anyone like that, and I can't do what they did." If you say this, then you are correct—you cannot. Did Moses go up to the Red Sea thinking, "I don't care what God says, crossing this river just cannot be done and this will be either foolhardy or embarrassing." No, stuck between river and approaching chariots, he went in with complete and utter faith.

For the meditation to work you need to believe that you are just as qualified as any of the past masters. After all, what did they have that was any different than you? Moses stuttered so much that Aaron was appointed his spokesperson. They were all children, with strange or typical childhoods, same as you and me. They all grew up with the usual range of intellects, average education for the day, friends and playmates, everything normal enough. The *only* difference is that one day they decided that they were capable of, or the conduit for, something astounding.

So, at the start, you need to tell yourself, "I can do this," and feel that fact with absolute certainty. Believe that you are just the same as Moses or Buddha. Imagine yourself with the spiritual power. Only then will you have access to it. Starting from there, we have some general steps to meditate on achieving a miracle.[1]

Find a quiet place free of distractions. Make sure that there are no phones, loud background noises, or people bugging you. Just a place where you can focus on yourself. It could be the top of a mountain, a beach, or simply your backyard if you live in a quiet neighborhood.

Remove yourself from the outside world. Think not of your daily stresses but focus on the spiritual. Forget entirely about the world outside. Meditating alone may also be best because having someone else around, even if they are meditating, could be distracting.

Many schools of meditation recommend some fasting before beginning. I would say at the least make sure you haven't eaten or drank anything in the two hours beforehand, but don't go into it starving. You really do not want to be interrupted by indigestion from your last meal. Also, don't do any drugs or alcohol. You want a clear and sober mind.

Sit in a relaxed, but alert position. The infamous lotus position is good for this, with your back straight and upright. And, do not be fooled. Sleeping is not meditating.

As you meditate, have your affirmations in mind. Tell yourself that you have the power to achieve, that you are calling upon it, and that you have importance. This can be in the form of a mantra, repeated phrase, a piece of scripture, or anything that works for you.

Then, keep in mind the miracle that you want; visualize it in your mind, and keep repeating to yourself that it will happen. Open your mind to the possibilities, to the Universe and to your higher self. You cannot make it happen unless you can *see* it happening in your mind's eye. Want to have a visitation from some angelic-like figure? Then you must visualize the point of light from which it will evolve. Need a problem solved? Then visualize its solution. Visualization is truly important. Depending on the particular school of meditation, you can meditate with eyes closed, or focused on something such as a flickering flame or small object; just make sure to keep your attention focused on one thing.

Believe in yourself. Believe in your higher spiritual self. Just as I have said, you must *know* that you can do this, and know that you have the power to make it happen. You are making this happen, so you must have no doubt as to its success. Whether it is a miracle or a vision, you must be certain that it will happen.

Be patient. It will happen, but some events take longer to initiate than others. You must simply have faith.

Expect a miracle. Expect it to happen. You must be completely resolute in your belief that it will come and have faith as to its inevitability. If you hear thoughts that are negative as you read this, I can tell you to not even bother with the exercise; it will not work unless you are convinced. You cannot fool the same intelligence that created you. It does not listen to language, it (god/universe whatever you want to call "it") responds to your consciousness, your brain wave, and your energy.[2]

Let's sum this up in a quick bullet-point list:

1. Find a quiet place.

2. Remove yourself from the outside world.

3. Fast; no drugs or alcohol.

4. Sit, relaxed but alert and focused.

5. Use your affirmations or mantra. Visualize. Focus with eyes closed or on small object.

6. Believe in yourself.

7. Be patient.

8. Expect a miracle and trust in yourself.

Meditate this way, focusing on your chosen miracle, and it will come. No matter which school of meditation, this quick summary seems to be the general methodology. Now let's see what the recommended way to *pray* for a miracle is.

How to Pray for a Miracle

Different religions have different ways of praying. Catholics drop to their knees before an altar, Muslims drop to their knees on a mat and face toward Mecca, and others drop to their knees before a statue or representation of their chosen deity. Well, maybe there's not much difference after all. Let's bring together the common elements of praying.

You need first to have a quiet place where you can focus on God, Allah, Brahma, or whoever it is. Usually this is a church or temple, but it could also be a little shrine you have in your home, or simply just the foot of your bed.

To focus on your miracle means to focus on God (by whichever name), and not the daily stresses of the outside world. You must remove mental noise so as to allow clarity of your thought or intention. So, to pray properly, you must remove yourself from the world around you. Again, a church or temple is good for this, but often simply someplace removed. *The Point of Power* book goes into a great deal of detail on this subject.[3]

Some religions state that you must fast before engaging in a prayer for something of true importance. If you go to mass, then it must be at least an hour since you last ate or drank. History records holy men fasting for several hours or days as they commit themselves to prayer. For the true believer who really wants his miracle, fasting is an important part of both religion and praying.[4]

Sit in supplication before God. Usually this means kneeling and bowing one's head. You want to stay alert though, keep your mind focused on God's presence and the miracle that you need, so no falling asleep.

Select a prayer, and then repeat it in a whisper or just to yourself. For Christians, the "Our Father" is a popular prayer, and I'm sure each religion has its favorites. Alternately, a selection of scripture that you feel is appropriate to your needs can be recited over and over.

Then visualize your needs and send them up to God; open your mind to God as you ask of Him your needs. Also recommended is to have some religious symbol to focus on; a cross, rosary, or prayer bead. Believe in God. If you expect God to grant your miracle, then you must believe that God can. Believe in God 100 percent, knowing that God *can* and *will* help you.

Be patient. God will work his miracle, but in God's own time and way. Just trust in God and wait.

And lastly, expect the miracle to happen. Know that God will come through for you and give you your miracle. Be totally resolute in your faith in God, and it will come.

Okay, now let us sum these steps to praying in a quick bullet-point list.

1. Find a quiet place.

2. Remove yourself from the outside world.

3. Fast; no drugs or alcohol.

4. Kneel before God; relaxed but alert and focused.

5. Use a prayer or selection of scripture. Visualize. Use a religious symbol to focus on.

6. Believe in God.

7. Be patient.

8. Expect a miracle and trust in God.

Pray this way, keep focused on God and what you need, and the miracle will come. Differences in scriptures, prayers, and ceremony aside, this seems to be the general outline for praying to the deity of your choice. It is the same way the various saints throughout history have prayed, the same way that Muslims pray to Allah, and the same way the ancient Greeks prayed to Zeus. The method never changes, but the details of it can change.

Comparison

So, now let us compare the two. See how different praying for a miracle is than meditating on one? Wait. Substitute "belief in God" for "belief in self," and they are the same basic actions. Both are a prayer to the Universe in some form, and both are asking of it to fulfill some need. Furthermore, history is filled with examples of religious or holy people that achieve miracles through prayer. Doing it by way of meditation instead of praying is simply a more generic variation; you are asking something of the Universe, but God *is* the Universe, so by meditating you are praying to God.

There is one more thing we need to compare here. This goes all the way back to *The Point of Power*. There we talked about the Law of Attraction, and how we can ask of the Source the fulfillment of our needs. Now let's see, how did that procedure go? Intend, Declare, and Detach.[5]

Or to elaborate…

1. You must find a quiet place where you can focus.

2. Remove yourself from the outside world. Forget your daily stresses lest they muddy your connection with the universe, and just keep focused on yourself and your need.

3. While fasting is not a requirement, keeping a clear mind is. So avoiding drugs or alcohol would be best. As far as food or water, just make sure you won't be interrupted by an unwanted call of Nature.

4. Stay relaxed but alert and focused. Sitting upright is a good way to do this. You should focus on your Intent alone. Intend.

5. Visualize. See yourself and your situation as you would like it to be and as though it has already happened.

6. Believe in yourself; believe that it can be done. Tell the universe that this is what you want, what you need. Declare.

7. Send the thought out into the universe; let it go. Detach and be patient and DETACH.

8. Expect it to happen, know that you will have your need or desire met, your miracle served like risotto at your favorite Italian restaurant.

Intend, Declare, Detach, and you will have your miracle. Hmm... This list looks kind of familiar. In fact, it's exactly the same. If you don't believe me, then go back and read through *The Point of Power* again. It would appear that the procedure for praying for a miracle, for meditating on a miracle, and for manifesting a miracle through our thoughts as we talked about in *The Point of Power* are all one and the same thing! Maybe there are more similarities than at first we thought. Ah, but in one we're praying to God or the universe which *is* God, while in the other we're...

You're getting ahead of me now; there is something else going on here. Our third section is therefore going to be a comparison, to see how our Quantum Mechanical viewpoint fits in with the ever-present God we all know of so well. Before you decrying that science and religion never mix or that I'm about to try and sink your faith—have no fear, you will find that both have been trying to tell us the exact same thing. Religion is simply the more poetic and less technical way of telling us what science spells out in elaborate detail. There is a God, by whichever name you know God as, and it will be science that tells us what God is. After knowing that, you just might gain more respect and appreciation for God's presence.

Chapter 13

MAGIC

We cannot talk about miracles of prayer, meditation, and manifesting without inevitably getting into the subject of magic, something many religions oppose. So let's be brave and tackle that one as well. We need a good definition of what magic is. Some people just say "magic is the Devil's work" and avoid it. Others like using science fiction's favorite quote about how a high enough level of technology is indistinguishable from magic.[1]

Magic Defined

The Wikipedia definition is: "Magic is the claimed art of manipulating aspects of reality, either by supernatural means or through knowledge of occult laws unknown to science." Whereas science does not blindly accept anything and subjects everything to observation and logical analysis, those who practice magic simply accept it as some inexplicable force and move on.

Others define magic as the art of creative consciousness, learning to apply our thoughts as a part of the creative flow of existence to create specific results. Furthermore, while some brands of magic do have elements of religion in them, the focus is more in achieving results than on religious worship.

The obvious definition just might be that magic is access to a force or power not yet understood by science. The psychological sciences do distinguish between magic and magical thinking, such as the belief that standing in front of a building, one must turn around three times in order to keep the roof from falling in. Such magical thinking is devoid of prayer, meditation, or positive visualization, but operates at the level of fear or compulsive behaviors.

Magic and Miracles

Tibetan monks can perform many a seeming miracle upon themselves. In the 1980s, one monk was documented on camera as being able to raise the temperature of his skin through meditation. Others are able to lower their metabolism by 64 percent, compared to a 10 percent to 15 percent drop when you sleep. In the icy cold wearing nothing more than their simple robes, they were able to sleep comfortably through the night, generating enough heat on their own not to die of hypothermia. Okay, definitely miracles, but not technically magic. We can categorize these as meditation miracles.[2]

Hinduism has texts in the Vedas that discuss both white and black magic, and many of their holy men (or *siddhars*) are said to be able to perform miracles that are ordinarily impossible to perform. Indeed Hinduism has a history of miracles being reported amongst its people. Is this evidence of magic or simply primitive cults?

In ancient Egypt, magic was used as a protection from angry spirits, ghosts, deities, demons, and evil sorcerers that were thought to cause their illnesses and misfortunes. This was tied into their religion, which some view as a primitive religious cult. Shamans the world over have the task of being the intermediary between ours and the spirit world, which naturally has them functioning as priests as well. This seems just like another cult.

Many ancient cults used magic in the form of ritual incantations, words spoken with some symbolic item held out before them, to banish a demon possessing a person, sanctify an area against the forces of evil, invoke a spirit to fulfill a request, or in some extreme cases perform miracles such as evading pursuers by parting a large section of water before them or creating wine out of water.

Christians will recognize the water-into-wine as Jesus' first miracle at the wedding in Cana. From the point of view of someone who knows nothing about either Christianity or, say, Shamanism, what is the difference between a shaman holding out his feather-covered magic stick to banish evil spirits, and a priest holding out a pair of crossed sticks with a carving of a dying man on it to banish the Devil? In both cases something symbolic is used, and in both cases words are uttered to send the demon or spirit away. One says a magic incantation, the other a prayer. One might invoke spirits while, the other invokes the Holy Spirit. There is much similarity between the two, except the names are different.

Then there are the shamans who do not invoke or worship a given deity or spirit at all, but simply attempt to call upon the essence of a thing itself, like the force of Nature or the Earth. If you use a magic amulet or a cross, then you are still using something to focus your belief and concentration into manifesting your desires. Blessed candles, holy water, sacred wafers of bread, blessed palm fronds or other plant parts—how many of these are objects of Christian worship and how many are objects of magic use? The obvious answer would be that all could be used for either purpose. So then, how much difference is there between prayer and magic?

The Church disallowed magic centuries ago; only the Church could perform it. If a saint, priest, or other holy person performed what amounted to magic, then it was a "miracle," but if a layman performed it then it was called magic and deemed sourced by the Devil, and hence evil. Prayer, holy miracles, and the like are merely official Christian magic. They have different rituals, different words, different symbolisms, but the same basic mechanism.

Magic as Direct Access

Practitioners of magic seek to access the patterns of creation directly, the realms of the natural and natural forces, while a prayer—of any religion—seeks to access these forces indirectly through the intermediary of a deity or spirit. In religious prayer it is belief in a higher power that counts while in much of magic practice it is belief in yourself and your own abilities that is key. Confidence, whether in a deity or in yourself, is the common element in both.

In prayer, one often asks for general good fortune or problems to be solved. Many are afraid to ask for something large or momentous for fear of being labeled "selfish" or "greedy," because they also desire such largess. In many magic rituals, the requests get rather specific, which is perhaps an aid in properly manifesting the desire? All the symbols, rituals, numerical patterns, and odd shaped runes are merely means used to specify the desire with a lot more detail and hence aid in achieving the proper focus. In the end, it all comes down to a proper mindset, anyway.

Mindset, Symbols, and Creativity

Magic can be said to have three components, which are mindset, symbols, and creativity. Symbols merely help the mind to focus in on the desire, much like praying before an altar or a cross. Creativity and imagination are needed to properly envision exactly what you want. Then finally the mindset; you must *believe* that what you are attempting is possible, and that it is going to have an effect in order for it to work. Without belief, prayer, manifestation, or what is known as magic, it will all fail to work.[3]

Some magic involves the use of herbal components. There are two different types of purposes for such. First, if they are symbolic of the desired result they fall under the "symbols" category, and second if the properties of the herbs have an actual physical effect on someone, they fall under chemistry and really don't involve our discussion of magic.

Symbols, of whatever form in magic, assist in getting the mind to believe that it can access some external power, so it really is a part of the "mindset." Like prayer and manifesting, magic is not possible without a firm belief. A lot of magic even involves the picturing of symbols in your mind, drawing the magic circles out mentally then casting them forth; again, mindset and creativity. For those not creative enough, the more physical symbols are used to help things along.

The desire is then to make contact with a higher plane, another reality, or other source of universal power flow. In most cases, this is represented by the so-called *Astral Plane*. That is a realm where magic power flows, spirits can be contacted, and desires manifested. It is a realm of thought and spiritual essence, a realm of creative force that stretches from star to star, where desires can physically manifest if one knows how.

Sounds sort of like that old Zero Point Field, doesn't it?

Witchcraft

Witchcraft is the realm of magic popularized with ugly ladies in pointy black hats doing unspeakable things for dark powers or sending flying monkeys after people. But, did you know that what we know as witchcraft was actually the craft of the healer? Back before Christian times, the local healers were the ladies who knew something about herbs and what to use to heal a wound. But, as other religions would later take over, the clergy liked being the ones to whom people came for help, so anything else was branded as "evil," particularly since "witchcraft" actually put women in charge. Men, of course, could have mastered the art of herbs, but way back in those times they were usually hunting for dinner.[4]

So, witchcraft as a field of magic comes down to that part which is basically chemistry and that part which is manifestation. Herbs, potions, and what they do are chemistry; any accusations beyond that are the result of paranoia and fear from a far more primitive time. That leaves the manifesting part, same as for any other type of magic.

Manifesting through Magic

So, how specifically does manifesting something work in magic? Well, on average the steps appear about the same, give or take some differing symbolisms, incantations, and methods.

1. First, you need a quiet place where you can focus, or a place where you won't be interrupted or distracted.

2. Second, you need to remove yourself from the outside world to connect with the magical one. This can be done by envisioning a glowing circle around yourself, or actually drawing one on the ground and using that to focus upon.

3. Next, you must keep a clear mind, focused on what you are about. A cloudy mind will prevent you from getting a good connection with the Astral or whichever realm of magical power you're calling upon.

4. The key to good magic, from many sources, is mental focus, so find a position to sit or stand that will keep you relaxed and focused throughout the ceremony.

5. As was said before, visualization is key. You must visualize your desires and every aspect of your magical process. If you seek to dispel a demon, you must picture him being physically tossed out; if you seek to heal someone, then you must visualize the healing beginning.

6. Belief is also key. Believe the magic will work, that the change will occur. Tell the Universe, or Astral, or whichever spirit power that you're calling upon, what you need.

7. Cast out your spell; send your need into the Universe.

8. Believe that it will happen, believe in the magic and that your spell will work.

Give or take some details, this is the general procedure. Some might use crystals to help achieve a proper resonance with what they desire, others use the drawing of symbols to help attract the correct vibrational energies, or ceremonial herbs for much the same effect, but it's all still the same basic method.

Does this list seem familiar? In the last chapter, I presented nearly the exact same list when comparing praying and manifesting. It would seem that magic not only holds many similarities with our main subject, but that it also is simply another name for what happens with prayer and manifesting.

Conclusion

So, back to our definition of magic: *Magic* is the name given to that which we as humans do not understand.

Do you remember Michael J. Fox's character, Marty McFly, in *Back to the Future*? Fox travels back 30 years to 1955, using his car, a Delorian. How could he do seemingly strange things? Magic.

Is magic the work of the Devil, or evil? Or, is it simply another way of accessing the same universal power that Prayer attempts to seek out, the same power that Manifesting attempts to focus on? I am convinced it's the latter. By any other name, it is still but a rose, or in this case the Zero Point Field.

Be it prayer, meditation, or even magic, it is all the same thing. Those are all processes to get you in the right mindset that you may generate your Faith Wave, and from there manifest your desires. By whichever name, it is a way of training your brain to go into this specific wave, which is the waveform that allows you access to the Zero Point Field, where dreams are made into reality.

Different approaches, but they all boil down to clearing the mind of the Ego and anything else trying to impose limits upon it, and then focusing on the here-and-now and what you want. Viewing that desire not as a pipe dream, but as an actuality that will *inevitably* happen.

Visualizing it. Knowing it. Feeling it.

Prayer, meditation, magic are all methods to achieve this state of mind, this Faith Wave. All methods for visualization, setting a clear intention, and having faith that the Universe, God, or whatever, will take care of it. All of these ancient practices involve the same process of starting with complete faith—in a deity, greater power, or yourself—and knowing that it will be done, focusing on your current need—be it in prayer, focused meditation, or ritual—then letting it go and awaiting for God or the Universe to see it done.

This process should sound rather familiar to you by now, of course, for I have covered it before, just with different names: Intend, Declare, and Detach.

Part Three

THE EXPLANATION

Chapter 14

SCIENCE VERSUS RELIGION

Religion and science are often seen as opposing one another. This impression comes largely as early scientists disrupted earlier views of the universe, especially those taken to be revealed. For example, Galileo believed in Copernicus's sun-centered solar system (1514), confirmed it experimentally—for example, ocean tides proved that the earth is in motion—and was tried for heresy (1633). In the West, from the middle ages to the modern period, this tension was often acted out. Only later did theologians view science as the uncovering of God's mysteries built into the Creation. And, as the last section shows, there is some exciting common ground after all.[1]

Science deals with facts, data, and the provable. It starts by coming up with a theory to fit observed data, then testing that theory to see how good a fit it makes, and how good it is at predicting what comes next. If the fit is bad, then the theory is modified and tested again. If the fit is really bad, then the theory may be abandoned until someone comes up with something better. It is a process that seeks to understand the way the Universe, the forces of Nature, and the processes of Reality works.

Religion, it is said, deals with faith. But, what do you have faith in, exactly? Faith in God? Faith in divine teachings? Faith in what was meant to be taught or faith in the exact way it was written down? Not as easy a question to answer as you might think. So let us begin by breaking down the various aspects of religion.

Science versus Morality

As we have seen earlier, religions over the world have a component of *morality*, which is "the differentiation of intentions, decisions, and actions between those that are good (or right) and those that are bad (or wrong)" (Wikipedia). A moral code is a system of teachings that tell you the proper way to behave toward yourself and one another. Nothing is in conflict with science there. In fact, science has absolutely nothing to say about morality because that is not the function of science. The function of science is to explain things, and not tell you how to behave. Science leaves that to religion and philosophy.

Science versus Religious History

For any given holy book—such as, the Torah, the Bible, and the Qur'an—a certain proportion of it reads as a historical account. The event was witnessed by actual people, and later recorded for subsequent generations. Nothing is in conflict with science here. In fact, science will often take some of these stories, use various methods to ascertain their accuracy, and search for details that might have been left out of the religious accounts. Here science and religion are not in conflict, they are working together for a common goal. Religious texts can be a place from which science can start as it delves deep into the past.

Let us dwell on this "point-of-view" matter for a moment because this is truly important. These various books form the cornerstone for one religious group or another. What we read in each was witnessed and recorded by an individual or individuals from their understanding or perspective. That is, each writer is a human with a human's flaws. The Great Flood in the Bible, for instance, is said to have encompassed the entire world; science calls such a claim ridiculous, but wait. What exactly was the world to the people of biblical times? They did not

not true

not true

know about North or South America, Australia, or for that matter most of Asia and Africa. Their entire world, was the region around the Mediterranean Sea. So for their entire world to flood, all you need is for something to occur to make just the Mediterranean Sea flood over (or maybe the sea used to be a lot lower before the Flood than it is now).

So, what was written long ago can be true, but the perspective of the writer who wrote it (in the case of the Flood, the tradition ascribes authorship to Moses many years later) needs to be taken into account, as well as for whom it was written (in the case of the Flood, if written by Moses, would be for the Israelites who were straying from God).

The Flood is a blatant example, but you get the idea. The world of the Creation story is a flat earth with water above the sky and water below the dirt, which can fall down, and bubble up, to overtake dry land at any time around which all the other solar bodies rotate.

On the matter of historical records, science and religion really have no disagreements, if both just remember that historical accounts from any ancient source can be peppered with inaccuracies and matters of perspective, or assumptions about the world and its nature.

In science and mathematics, it is called setting up your "initial conditions." In this case, if your initial condition is the statement, "The entire world flooded over completely," then you will never find any evidence to support such a proposition; all you have to do is discover a complete lack of evidence for flood waters in the Andes or Himalayas. But, if your initial condition is the statement, "The entire ancient world of the Mediterranean Sea flooded over," then you just might find enough supporting evidence.

Science versus Religious Law

The commandments set down by ancient theocracies are another component of those religions. Such commandments tell you what to eat, how to act, and how to maintain cleanliness. Are those really things handed down by God? Are they an essential part of the religion and its message? Think back to ancient times and what was going on, and how some nations were ruled.

"*Theocracy* is a form of government in which the official policy is to be governed by immediate divine guidance or by officials who are regarded as divinely guided, or simply pursuant to the doctrine of a particular religious sect or religion" (Wikipedia).

Many primitive societies were theocracies either with religious leaders in charge or highly consulted. For example, on Mount Horeb, God appointed Aaron (Moses' brother) to be Moses' assistant; later, God appoints Aaron and his lineage to become the priest class in the tradition. When God is directing things, then the people (the nation, the cultus) find it difficult to argue. And how were they to know any different? These common folk were peasants or farmers or sheepherders or laborers without an education or even time to learn. Learning was left to the rulers and the clergy (who often were the educators for the ruling class).

"Is this animal good to eat?" When such a question came up, it likely was answered on one of two levels. The first level is the general prohibitions about eating some kinds of things, such as the Jewish law against eating animals unless they had completely cloven hooves and were ruminants. We know now that a pig, for instance, is about the most parasite-ridden animal you can eat if not cooked properly. So God's law is entirely reasonable on a public health standpoint.

The second level is implementation or detail work. In the case of pigs, how reasonable would it be to say to persons several thousand years ago, you may each eat pork, but "only if the pig is properly cooked to a temperature of at least 350 degrees for at least 20 minutes per pound." Safer to just ban it. Jewish priests still inspect cattle being slaughtered and the assessments used from several thousand years ago are still used by the U.S. Department of Agriculture as a measure of whether a cow can become human food.

Ancient clergy had to juggle both matters of religion and state, much as Muslim Taliban continue to do in Afghanistan and other countries. Their statements came from those trusted with the religious and communal welfare. The theological leaders didn't mind; the people listened to them, did what the clergy knew would keep them healthy, and then they could move on with the more important matters of their religious worship.

Regarding these matters, does science have any objection or opposition? Of course not. In fact, in our more technically aware society, science has confirmed a few of them and told us the specific reasons behind them, for example in the kosher laws.

Science versus Religious Science

We are left with the parts where science and religion *do* seem to come in conflict. *Infallibility*, as used in Christian Catholic theology, denotes the preservation from error of the church, a general council, or the pope. (*Indefectibility* is the more general protection by the Holy Spirit, that despite human weakness, the church will remain the church.) *Inerrancy*, as used in Christian Evangelical theology, denotes the truth of each sentence of the Bible as well as the truthfulness of the entire corpus. Popes have ruled as follows or theologians have read the Bible to mean:

— "God created everything" whereas science speaks of evolving species.
— "The world is only 5000 years old" whereas science says "it's actually billions of years old"
— "The World was created in seven days" whereas science says "it's more like a hundred million years"
— "God created Man in God's own image" whereas science says, "Humanity evolved"

— "Man may have written down the Book, but it was God himself who put the words in each writer's mind" whereas science says "Many different writers have rewritten or edited passages" and "Moses is surely not the author of the Torah"

Yet, not all of it is irresolvable. Remember, the clergy were the only educated people in their day, the only ones capable of studying any of such matters. It was their job to explain things in the simplest manner possible for the peasants to grasp it. And even then, there were things that went far beyond what the clergy of the day could comprehend themselves. The solution? Enter the "parable."

In the Christian New Testament, Jesus uses parables to explain several moral concepts to the people, so they might better understand what he was saying. A parable is what we would call a metaphor in story form. It tells something in terms more easily understood, and then ends by comparing that to the point being taught. The mustard seed, for instance, was a favorite parable. It is a tiny seed that grows into a large plant, which Jesus would then compare to the spread of his teachings. The number of followers starts out small, but later grows into something huge.

The Hebrew Bible, Qur'an, and other holy books also use parables and metaphors. These were the only ways to make the peoples of five thousand years ago understand concepts that would have bogged down their understanding of the key religious teachings, which had to do more with morality, God, and the power of prayer.

So, what is left between science and religion? First, some things often held as true by the faithful do no appear in the Bible or anyone else's holy book. These are things that humans later derived on their own based on what they thought they knew of the Bible, or other holy book.

For instance, the age of the world—some believers say it's slightly over 5000 years old while science has mounds of data to say that it's a whole lot older. These believers claim that each day of Creation is a

Not true

Yom, a 24-hour day. Several of the patriarchs have listed their ages at death and, with a little detective work, an age is added up. *Methuselah 900 fiery*

So let me do a little detective work as well. The lifespans get shorter as human sin grows, until finally God floods the known world, saving Noah and only seven other people in the ark. Then God repents of such destruction and seeks to assist a people. And yet, nowhere in the Bible does it give a calendar date for Creation. Nowhere does it say "this happened 5000 years ago."

Take the whole "created in seven days" thing. Science will tell us about gas clouds millions of light-years across condensing over a hundred million years into a collection of millions of smaller denser clumps, which then ignite to become stars while the debris around them spends a few extra million years to form into worlds. The worlds then cool, and over another hundred million years conditions might become right for the first microorganisms to form, leading to the eventual evolution of something like humanity.

Two equally enchanting stories without eye witnesses. Now which story would you like to use to explain this to some farmer from four or five thousand years ago? You'll lose him the first time you say "million" as he tries to comprehend what that is. (Come to think of it, I have little sense of a million years!) You could spend months trying futilely to explain it to him, during which time he'll just lose interest and never get around to the part about seeking justice and loving kindness. Even God would say, "Okay folks, it's like this. I created everything in seven days" though even here one might suspect the original term might be better translated as seven "generic time periods." One might also note that many of the body's biological rhythms happen to fall into a seven day cycle, and that's maybe why that number of 'days' for Creation was chosen.

Or take Evolution. Do you really want to explain molecular biology and genetics to someone whose entire understanding of science amounts to "tree pretty, fire bad?" Just telling humans of long ago that

"God created humanity," was enough to get the point across and just leave out all the messy details for now. When humanity is ready to know, then they'll figure it out for themselves.

So, even at this greatest of divides between religion and science, or between faith and reason, is there really that much of an irresolvable disagreement? Or, have they both been talking about the same things all along just on different levels? In matters such as these, science and religion may just be two sides of the same coin (another parable, or metaphor). Just like Relativity is said to be the more complex version of the old Newtonian Laws, only as they apply as we approach the speed of light, so too would science be the more complex explanations for what some aspects of what religion has sought to explain. It would seem that science and religion aren't so incompatible after all.

Ah, but faith and the power of prayer have no worldly explanation, or nothing of science about it. But, think back to the rest of the book. Unless you are intending on keeping a measure of conflict inherent in the nature of religion (which some people seem determined to do), science and religion can find common ground. In fact, this has been the whole point of this entire book.

Science versus Prayer

We have seen that quantum mechanics leads us to believe that we can manifest changes into our reality. Prayer and meditation can also manifest changes into our reality, as documented over the centuries by various accounts of miracles. Manifesting, as we explained in *The Point of Power*, requires a focused state of mind and absolute faith that it will happen. Prayer and meditation also put one into a focused state of mind, and require absolute faith that what you pray for will happen. Manifesting requires a belief in your access to the Zero Point Field; prayer requires belief in God to access God's power.

The parallels are too close to just ignore them. We have but one conclusion that we can make here. Prayer and meditation are the same as manifesting. Thoughts can manifest into our reality, change it, and direct it to what we need and want. Prayer, or meditation, is but a form of directed thought that accesses the exact same influence over our reality. It is not a coincidence, not something that theology was unaware of and just happened to bump into in the course of worship, but rather something that was intentionally there all along. Another parable, another thing that needed to be put into far simpler terms that the average peasant could understand.

Even now, we are just beginning to understand the implications of quantum mechanics and what it is telling us, so could you really expect typical Bronze Age persons to come close to grasping any of this? Of course not. Far easier to tell him to pray to God to get what you need. If you are pure of soul, then God will grant it... Or, if your focus is pure, if there are no doubts in your mind that what you want is right, then ask God.

Think about it. We are raised with enough morals that if we have any doubts that something we want or need might not be just or right, than our subconscious will realize this and cause enough internal disagreement to mess up the signal we put out; in essence, we judge ourselves. This is just as God would judge us.

Manifesting and prayer is the exact same thing; one is merely a simpler statement of the other. That just leaves the one last part of the puzzle. Manifesting is something you do on your own to access the Zero Point Field while praying is done to a universal deity to fulfill one's wishes.

Chapter 15

WHAT IS GOD

Before we go any further, let us first define what God means in the various worlds' religions. Now, for convenience sake, we use *God* to refer to whichever supreme deity to whom someone may be referring, be it Yahweh, Allah, Brahma, or Enlightenment. Whenever you see the word *God*, then read this as your sense of the Divine. I do this for more than convenience; each of the world's major religions defines God as all-powerful universal Being. I take it that they each are referring to the same ultimate reality.

Two religions seem foreign to the notion of God, namely, Shinto and Buddhism. We treat these first.

Shinto

Shinto has multiple gods or (more correctly) spirits. Everything has a spirit including plants, animals, and places. The greater Kami is what we call the gods, and Amaterasu Omikami rules over them all. When a person dies, his spirit becomes another kami. Because a place can also have its own spirit, or kami, a more correct translation of *kami* might be "spirit force." You will find it in rocks, plants, rivers, mountains, the sun, animals, and ancestral spirits. It is both spirit and natural force, and does not reference God in the same as other world religions.

Yet, Shinto believers are essentially describing a universal spirit force of which each kami is a part. If you want to term their collective presence as a supreme Deity, in that sense you would not be wrong. This universal spirit force thus pervades everything and everyone—the entire world and by extension all the stars above and well beyond. The collective of the myriad of the kami encompass the entire universe.

Buddhism

At the time of Enlightenment, I become the Buddha; I become God with all the other Enlightened Beings. We are One.

Hinduism

For Hinduism, the supreme one is Brahma, and from him springs dharma, or the universal principle of law, order, harmony, and truth. Dharma is the regulatory moral principle of the Universe, while Brahma is the universal spirit or the universe itself. From him, the world and the universe spring. He is more than the supreme deity. He is the universal Force.

Now, each person is said to have a soul, or Atman. According to some Hindu theologies, *Atman* is indistinguishable from the universal spirit of Brahma, and the goal of life is to realize that one's Atman is identical to Brahma. In other words, we each have a piece of God in us, each of us is a part of God, and God pervades everything, everywhere. There is only one spirit, or spirit force, and that is Brahma, and we are each a part of Brahma.

Part of this sounds similar to Shinto; by just substituting Atman for Kami (and keeping in mind the myriad of the Kami), one could name the collective Brahma. The two religions are far apart in other respects.

Hinduism, however, seems open to such convergent thinking. One statement in the annals of Hinduism maintains that there is only one God, who is known by different names to different people.

Not True

Abrahamic Religions

Abrahamic religions, as we have grouped them, refer collectively to all religions that spring from the common ancestor of Abraham: Judaism and its descendants Christianity, Islam, and a myriad of lesser-known variations. By definition, they all worship the same God, but use their own languages to pronounce the name. *Allah*, Arabic word, means "God" in English, just as *Yahweh* in Hebrew means "God" in English. So, languages aside, *God* is the same entity for each of these religions. Differences between each of these religions and their teachings are secondary from this over-arching unity.

In this family of religions, God is the Creator who made Heaven and Earth, all the stars, and any other world there might be. The world and the universe literally sprang from God's power, so one might say God is the Universe and all of Creation. From God's Being, all existence springs.

Even in Wicca (a form of paganism), while they have two major deities, they regard "the whole cosmos as alive, both as a whole and in all of its parts." Thus, we all agree that there is only the one God; we just disagree on the details of God's name and what God stands for.

God Defined

So, it would seem that all the world's major religions have the one commonality, namely, the similar enough conception of the supreme deity. God for all comes down to one entity, an entity that not only created the entire Universe but also by definition is the entire Universe. The Universe is alive, and it is God.

Prayer

We have seen that prayer is a focused state of mind, exactly the same as what we saw in *The Point of Power,* being required to manifest our thoughts into reality. Prayer is the act of directed brain waves interacting with the Zero Point Field. This is exactly what quantum mechanics explains. But, prayer is supposed to be a communication to God that is performed with the purpose of asking Him for our needs to be fulfilled. And Manifesting is a communication to the Zero Point Field.[2]

There is only one conclusion that we can draw at this point. Either God is connected to the ZPF, or God *is* the ZPF. Does this mean that God is nothing more than a set of equations? Of course not. Any equation in science is merely used to arbitrarily define what something is, in a defined context and so these quantum mechanical equations allow us to also *define* what God is. But remember; these same equations demand there be an interaction of intelligence with the ZPF, which means that God *is* the Zero Point Field.

The Zero Point Field is everywhere, in everything, and all throughout the entire Universe. Quantum mechanics states this quite clearly. It connects everything with one another, and it is the vibe and pulse of all matter and spirituality. This also happens to be what all the world's major religions agree to be the definition of God. God *is* the Universe, all universes, God *is* the Zero Point Field, and God is within everything. God is in you and me, in the rocks and the trees, in every star… just as the Zero Point Field is.

God, Religion, and the Zero Point Field

So, I suppose a bit more exposition is required at this point. If indeed all religions are actually worshiping the same supreme deity, then why are there any differences at all? Cultural nuances and differing languages aside, why all the hostility over religious differences? Especially so, if they aren't really all that different?[3]

The answer is simple, and makes for a good one-liner: God created humans, and humans created religion.

It's like a group of blind men each grabbing hold of a different part of the elephant trying to guess what sort of animal it is. Throughout history, every religion and philosophy has sought after a part of the answer, and then interpreted it in the context of their own cultural viewpoint. Add in the local moral code and dietary restrictions and you have people thinking that all religions are different enough to fight over. Seems silly now, doesn't it? But wait, the differences get even sillier.

Remember, we just said that God is the ZPF, that God is everything that arises from it, which is to say everything—including you and me. Just as we are all connected through the ZPF, so too is there is a piece of God in every one of us. God cares for us because we are all a part of God's Being in the more literal scientific sense. Care about yourself, and the power of God or the ZPF will flow through you.

Matter is made up of energy, and energy is information energy is force, and energy is all connected through the Zero Point Field. But, the ZPF is more than just the background of this one single universe. If you view a given universe, or parallel reality, as having its own frequency of sorts, then there must exist an infinite number of such universes each at its own frequency, all of which connect up to its own ZPF. But, are these separate ZPFs? Or are they one and the same? If each Universe arises from a soup of energy at a given dimensional frequency, then this soup must have energies at all such frequencies in the same way that a collection of photons of differing frequencies can all exist in the same space and react with one another. This soup must then be the same source for all such universes. So, there is only one ZPF that is the source of not only our universe but also all universes and all parallel realities. There is one ZPF for an infinite variety of universes of infinite physical extent. There is one ZPF, and there is one God.

And, we're all a part of it all.

Now, before you start thinking intelligent design versus evolution, let me just say that God doesn't need to do it that way and God doesn't need to micromanage. Just as we can walk, think, and talk about our job while also not needing to concentrate on our blood pumping and liver working as well, so here does God not need to focus on the details of how such things as Life arises. The Laws of Nature make for a perfect automatic process to carry that out while God goes about the main Divine purpose. Of course, being a part of God, we have access to these same Laws of Nature, which arise from what God is, and can manipulate them using manifestation, prayer, meditation, magic, whatever you wish to call it.

So, if the ZPF is God, and God is consciousness, then all matter and energy arise from consciousness and pure thought. This implies, of course, that consciousness can also change what has arisen from it, which is what we have been discovering through this and previous books.

As we have discovered, the ZPF records everything happening upon itself, every action and word. This is important for the consideration of such concepts as Karma or "As you sow, so shall you reap." Every act you ever did is still vibrating its consequences throughout the ZPF, and going through an automated cause and effect process until it comes back to you again, for good or bad. Thus, the idea of cleaning up one's karma is an attempt to counteract the more negatively produced reverberations you sent out into the ZPF. Your actions will have their effects upon yourself and others, which is where the concepts of sin, karma, and similar ideas of morality come in. Of course, negative actions can also include negative thoughts. Think negatively about *yourself*, and we know what happens. You send out a negative request and invite misfortune upon yourself. If you're going "Hey, I'm not worth anything, so just hit me with your worst shot," then the Universe, ZPF, God, whatever, will shrug and reply "Okay, if that's what you want." Actions and thoughts or feelings have consequences, be it in religion or the physics of the ZPF.

Then to the religious question, "Why does God need to follow any sort of physical laws?" the answer should now be obvious. God does not *follow* the physical laws, for God *is* the physical laws. They arise out of what God is, and they are the way in which God interacts with us. So, do science and religion always have to be in direct opposition?

Of course not. In fact, science and religion can walk hand in hand like two sides of the same coin.

Believe in God, believe in yourself, and believe in the ZPF. It's all the same thing in the end; all that matters is *belief*. (By this, I mean an activity, not subscription to a set of doctrines; faith doesn't have a verb form.) With belief and faith in *something*, you can manifest your desires, change your reality, and manipulate energy and matter.

Chapter 16

BELIEF VERSUS IMAGINING

Belief in something, be it through prayer or focusing on the science of it, is key. But, is there a difference between believing in something, and simply imagining what it would be like? Actually, there is, and it's a key difference.

When you imagine something, you picture it in your head, and try to feel what having that object of your desires would be like. You observe the possibility with no emotions engaged and just run the virtual scenario through your mind. Ideally, you are acting like a computer or recording device; dreaming up the result, then putting in enough factual details to make it come into being.[1]

Belief is all emotion based which is a fine thing for when a positive emotion is involved. Unfortunately the presence of a positive emotion opens up the possibility of future intrusion of a negative one. Belief in a God, or in yourself, automatically leaves you open to the doubt. What if God won't listen? What if I can't do this by myself? The belief turns in upon itself, and then doubt becomes a self-fulfilling prophecy. Belief and faith are great when you engage the right emotional content, and when your feelings toward it are all positive, but if you, let in the negative feelings, the doubts, it will turn against you.

Not that pure imagining is entirely free of emotional bias, either. You begin to believe, emotionally feel that it can happen, and then...what?

If you can *feel* that it can happen, then you can also realize the possibility that it will *not*. Negative emotions enter in and the self-doubt pollutes your call out to the cosmos. Imagining becomes belief, which may become a belief that it *won't* happen.

But, perhaps that is where belief in a supreme deity comes in. A supreme infallible figure will never fail you, but will always listen, so it keeps the emotion of your faith pure. If what you want to manifest is slow in coming, then the other side of it enters. You then begin to think that God might be punishing you, and that you are unworthy. After all, aren't we all taught that we are unworthy? Every religion teaches some form of either original sin or bad karma, or some aspect of the religion where there is a reason why you are unworthy of God's gifts, and that is where the emotional doubt can come in. But, if God, the ZPF, or whatever you want to call it, is so willing and ready to hear your call, why would God ever tell us that we are unworthy? If indeed we are all a *part* of God, then we are worthy of being listened to just by that single fact. So, what gives?

The answer was given earlier. God created humanity, but *humans* created religion, and religions the world over have leaders who often have a desire to *remain* leaders. The way they do that is by creating a need for their presence within the general population, and altering the true message the various ancient religious and philosophical texts have been trying to relate.

So, who *is* worthy of God's gifts? Everyone. There are enough moral teachings available that if something you want to do is truly wrong then some part of you deep down will realize it and cancel out the call. Other than that, you are a part of the flow, a part of the universal Being, and therefore worthy of being heard and channeling its power. Period. If you can't manage enough belief and faith to make this work, then try it from a purely imaginative point of view and leave emotion out of the equation altogether. Negative emotions muddying up your broadcast is why many people fail at this.

Visualizing uses your mind and your imagination. Belief and faith are entirely emotion based, and that can be a powerful tool in manifesting your desires, but only *if* your belief remains positive. It is not enough to believe in a God who is ready to grant your needs. You must also believe yourself worthy enough to be listened to. In this regard, you are your own judge.

This is an interesting thought. No one else judges you, but God. Yet, you are a part of the ZPF, which means that you are a part of God. So, if you are the one judging yourself, then it is God who is judging you *through* you. No false modesty here, either. "God rewards the meek," so someone starts to act meek thinking that by punishing themselves God will listen, but somewhere in the back of their heads it's got to be occurring: the very act of *trying* to act meek, automatically means that you are not. And what good does punishing yourself for, say, being unsuccessful in something? You just start yourself on this great big downward emotional spiral, which gets you to believing that no good can come to you and so it does not.

Just be honest to yourself and the Universe and negative emotion will stay well away. Perhaps something like, "God, I'm not the best person, but I really need this, and I think that I am worthy of it." The ZPF really appreciates honesty.

— Visualizing: That new car would look great in the driveway, and it's something I've needed too.

— Faith: Don't worry, I *will* get that car; I don't know how, but it will happen!

— Negative emotions polluting in: Oh, it would be *so* great to have that car, but that's never going to happen; I just don't have that sort of luck, and I can't afford it anyway.

See the difference? Emotions and feelings can both help and hinder in manifesting. If coupled with a strong enough belief in a higher power standing by ready to grant your needs, then it can be a good thing. But, even there you are telling yourself that God will only grant what you really need and anything else is being selfish. That gets into a game of convincing yourself that everything you could ever want is just a selfish request that won't get granted. But what constitutes "selfish" in a universe of infinite potential? Harking back to a previous chapter, I think it boils down to the Golden Rule, of which everyone has a version. Play nice with your neighbors, don't wish them harm or loss, and it will all be good. Beyond that, I don't think it's selfish to desire that new car, or even wanting to become a famous author. Your desire might just be the surface of some much deeper need. Perhaps, that new car is a symbol of the freedom you wish you had, or perhaps the desire for being a world famous author is because you really do have something to say that you feel the world should hear.

Don't judge, just imagine. Visualize it.

Even the Bible tells us to be like a child in order to enter God's kingdom. Perhaps something more was meant? A child has no limits of disbelief, for those are only later imposed by society. Anything a child can think of is possible. But, as we observed previously, all the child lacks is focus; she can imagine it, believe in it, but will soon find something else to focus on a few minutes later. She has not yet acquired the discipline that is needed. A child at play does not judge, she just imagines, visualizes, and believes. It's like believing in Santa Claus, but what if you could make old Santa *real?*

The data of everything that has ever happened, everything that ever was or could be, is stored within the ZPF like a sort of holographic data storage device. It is up to you to shift your focus within this hologram to a position where you can imagine the present that you most desire. The imagination can do it, but you must separate your ego and emotions. Emotions are a result of your interaction with the environment around you whereas the environment is the cause that you are trying to change. Focus on the emotions, and you focus on the effect instead of the cause.

Religious faith can be a useful tool for allowing you to manifest reality by giving the ZPF a more personal image to focus on, but beware of others manipulating your faith. Emotions cannot only be used by yourself to empower your call to manifest but can also be used by others for their own needs as well. How many holy wars throughout history have been guided by the desires of the very few by using the religious faith and emotions of the many? How many have preached something like, "Do this or God will *smite* you!" to induce fear enough to move a congregation to their own selfish needs?

Are your beliefs, religious or otherwise, your own or someone else's? Take away the emotional content for a bit and *then* start to visualize. See if what is around you is really for your own good or another's. Belief and faith are fine, but only if they are your own, and only if the emotion involved is purely positive. If you seek a better way to draw the line, then remember this: religions were invented by humans often to control others through fear, while pure faith in a higher power, that is here to help, is a purely positive viewpoint. The rest are simply details.

Religious beliefs can provide a moral compass as well as a figure (we are certain cannot fail us) to cling to in times of trouble. Something for our manifesting minds to gather strength and confidence around.

So, am I saying that all matters of faith and belief are negative and inferior to pure imagination? No, not at all. Just as a lot of religious teachings seem to be based on fear, some are based more on a belief in the self and in getting what you need, more than prostrating yourself before an altar purely for the sake of prostrating. What you have to do is look way back to the source material, and I mean really look.

Take the Christian Bible, for instance. "Whatsoever you desire, believe you have received it, and you will." Just repeat that slowly to yourself, and then think about it. That is word for word *exactly* what we have been talking about with the ZPF and manifesting. It is just given in words that the common folk of a few thousand years past could comprehend. The word "believe" could have been used simply because it was the easiest way of phrasing it for the people of the time. The goal was to get them started then a lot of preaching would be inserted to keep their beliefs channeled in a positive enough direction for the manifesting to work.

Pure imagining is factual, and unable to be cluttered by bad emotions. Faith and belief are highly emotion based, which can be good but only if it doesn't backfire on you. There is some crossover, however. Believe in something strongly enough, have enough faith, so that over time you see your efforts rewarded time and again, and that emotional-based belief turns into a logically based factual knowing. Take addition, for example. At what point in your very young childhood did you go from "believing" in a sum to "knowing" that the sum of two plus two equals four. To know it as a fact without having to psyche yourself up to be certain of it?

When imagining turns into absolute certainty, then it becomes pure faith, and pure faith can allow you to invoke your desires from the great cosmic being of the ZPF. Looking back, though, it would seem that is what portions of such ancient texts as the Bible were trying to teach us in the first place. Now we have quantum mechanics to show us the science behind it all.

Chapter 17

TIBETAN MONKS

We have made mention of the Tibetan monks before, and their seeming propensity for miracles of youth and long health. Well known for their appearance, pleasant attitude, and longevity, it is not unusual to find a monk who looks to be around forty years old to actually be in his eighties. So, what exactly is their secret? How do they stop the aging clock? Maybe there are a few things here that we should check into.[1]

Diet

The first obvious thing to ask would be, "What do they eat?" Many centuries before modern diet plans and scientific research into food, they had developed their own special diet. Though, as it turns out, it is not so much a diet but a *way* of eating, and knowing what types of foods to combine with what. If this sounds suspiciously like the modern concept of "food combining," or even Jewish kosher practices then you're right.

They have long stated that certain classes of foods should be eaten separately lest they combine in the stomach to cause not only digestion problems but a shortening of the life span. For instance, starches, fruits, and vegetables should be kept to a separate meal from meats, fish, and fowl. That starches clash with proteins is well known today, but the monks of Tibet had been saying it a whole lot earlier. Eat bread with meat—a sandwich—and a reaction is started in the stomach to cause discomfort. Don't eat carbohydrates with proteins and acidic fruits in the same meal. Eat proteins, starches, and fats in small quantities, and the main part of your diet should be veggies, salads, and fruits. Butter is neutral and can be eaten with starches or proteins, while milk mixes better with meat. Eggs are okay, but they note that the yolks are used by the brain and tissues while the whites are only used by the muscles and so should not be eaten unless you are about to engage in heavy physical labor.

The recommendations end with what amounts to your mother's advice: chew your food slowly and thoroughly before swallowing. That way your digestive system will be able to get the most nutrition out of it.

Most of this dietary advice sounds very similar to what we are discovering today, though perhaps rediscovering would be a better term, given that these monks had figured this out much earlier. It should be noted that while most monks are vegetarians, their diet does not entirely preclude meat. They will consume cheese and dairy products, and if they do have meat, it is eaten only in conjunction with which other foods it properly mixes; some meals may have a meat-only theme to best benefit digestion. Of course, the one notable point in the monk diet is that they eat only what they need; no overindulgence.

The secrets of the monks' diet, and their daily exercises coming up next, first made it to the outside world in the 1930s when Peter Kelder met with a British Colonel, who had apparently stayed in Tibet for a while with the monks. He brought back with him not only details on the way they eat as a means to stay young but also described a series of yoga-derived exercises called The Five Rites.

Exercise The Five Rites

The Five Tibetan Rites are a series of exercises said to be over 2,500 years old. They were derived from a series of even older yoga exercises when the monks of the time sought to narrow some twenty yoga positions down to a more limited selection of those they would consider as absolutely necessary. The goal of the five rites was to keep your *charkas* in balance. Chakras are a series of points around the body that together regulate the flow of your energy. They also happen to correspond to the locations of the endocrine glands, which are in charge of hormone regulation. Current medical research is pinpointing these glands as being key to aging (or not). These exercises, then, have the goal of activating these glands and keeping the energy flowing smoothly through your body.

Like any good yoga-derived exercise, breathing is important. It should involve long slow deep breaths and be done only through the nose. Together with the rites, endocrine gland performance is maximized; a key to good health and longevity.

A quick summary of the Five Rites starts with what is popularly known as the "Whirling Dervish." Stand with arms outstretched, even with the shoulders, and then spin around left to right until you become slightly dizzy.

The second rite involves lying down on your back, arms and hands flat to the sides. Then, while keeping legs straight and parallel raise them up until they are perpendicular to the floor, after which slowly lower them again. This is repeated.

For the third rite, you kneel on the floor, hands at the sides, palms flat. Then lean forward as far as you can while bending at the waist, head with chin on the chest. After that, you are to lean back as far as you can, causing the head to move as far back as you can while using your toes to prevent you from falling. End with coming back to an erect position, and then repeat.

The fourth rite is also known as one variation of "the Bridge" in yoga. You start off by sitting erect on the floor, legs stretched out in front, and perfectly straight. Hands are placed on the rug, chin on the chest, head forward. Then, gently raise the body while bending the knees, so that the legs from the knees to feet are vertical while the best of the body is horizontal. Your head falls back as you rise up, and your hands and feet now support you. It looks somewhat like a table facing to the sky. This is held before dropping back down and readying yourself to repeat.

The final rite, in yoga terms, is going from the down-dog position, scoop-diving down and curving up into the up-dog position. For the non-yoga types out there, the details are as follows: Hands and feet are on the floor about two feet apart, legs step back in line with the hands, while raising up your hips. You should look like a human triangle now, supported on your hands and feet. Next point, put your head down as if diving with the core of your body, hip following along last until the chin barely brushes the ground, and then straighten out until your legs are stretched out horizontal, but make sure that the chest and the stomach are stretching up vertically, supported on your hands, and head finally looking up. Hold this for a moment or two then reverse, going back into "down-dog" with your hips sticking up. This too is repeated a few times.

These then are the Five Rites. They are simple, easy to do, and proponents claim a number of benefits, including improved eyesight, memory, hair growth, anti-aging, and others. Though some state that such claims are exaggerated, all agree that there will be increased strength, flexibility, and energy. But, what then of those youthful-looking ancient monks? How do they do it, and is there more? Well, like most things you have to look at the entirety of the situation, the full range of variables that enter into things.

Rituals

Tibetan monks have many rituals. Some of these rituals are oriented toward some aspect of their meditation and others not so much. The Mandalla, for example. It is an elaborate geometric design, painted by four monks through the delicate and time-consuming placement of colored grains of sand. The result, many hours later, is a design three or four feet across that contains many concentric circles, a picture of a temple, stylized scrollwork, and a lot of intricate detail. Its purpose is to collect positive energies into itself and the area around it. Once finished, it is but a minute before the monks then destroy it, dumping its sands, and the positive energy they contain into a nearby lake or river to distribute the energies it has gathered. That is a painstaking ritual to demonstrate the impermanence of all things.

Another type of ritual involves bell-like sounds. The "Singing Bowls" are metal bowls that when filled with water resonate with a certain pitch. Then, there are the tiny metal symbols, each of which strikes a pitch that will wake you up and bring you right into the Present. The purpose of both of these, as well as other similar instruments, is not for music, but meditation. Certain sounds combined with meditation are said to be a very potent combination. But, we know this already. Think back a couple of chapters to *binaural beats;* the correct combination of sounds can set up the right frequency wave in the brain to better enable it to "be one with the universe" as some would say, or "connect with the ZPF," as we would say. Such binaural beats can increase one's theta waves, which are always good for a fit mind, and a fit mind leads to a fit body.

Buddhist rituals can revolve around meditations, contemplation of any of the moral precepts of Buddhism, the nature of Life and Afterlife, the soul, and more. In fact, like many other religions and belief systems around the world, such rituals would seem to all have a single common purpose.

Any ritual, if done with full awareness of the act that you are performing, and not just mindless droning with your mind wandering off, has the end result of bringing one's attention to a single point. In a Catholic mass, for instance, what is the real purpose of having the mass at all? How about other ritualistic acts that you perform? Muslims have their own rituals involving prayer mats facing toward Mecca, and for a dozen other religions there are hundreds of other rituals, all of which are usually done by people giving no thought to their meaning and purpose.

This is not the case for Tibetan Monks. Their belief is their core, and when they perform any of their rituals they do so with full awareness of what they are doing, the way they are doing it, and what sort of end result they expect. They are fully aware of the ritual and the reason. and that is the difference.

The purpose of any religious-seeming ritual is to bring one's *belief* to a focus; thereby properly attuning the brain's waveforms. It is not about worshiping something, about a tradition, or about anything save getting someone to really believe he/she can do whatever it is that he is meditating upon; Reaching the "Faith Wave." As we are seeing, in the belief lies power.

What is it that your average monk is trying to focus upon? They would call it "attaining Enlightenment," but we require a harder definition. What exactly is enlightenment? Various viewpoints would boil it down to connecting up with some sort of universal flow or power, not having to worry about, or experience, sickness and pain again, and transcending the body to remove one's self from the cycle of death and rebirth.

But lost in that quick list of philosophical overtones is a core belief amongst the monks that perhaps they do not voice often enough because they consider it so fundamental, just as you and I consider the act of breathing basic enough to not bother mentioning it to anyone. It is a belief that is supported by the nature of their rituals, bolstered by their exercises and diet, and proven every time one of them looks in a mirror. Every once in a while one of them will say it out loud, usually when outsiders are around, and they perhaps realize that such uninitiated people might not yet get it, although it is obvious.

But, what *is* that core belief that surrounds rituals to reaffirm and instill it into their very being? Simple. Aging is not normal. *Aging is not normal!*

Surrounded by rituals designed to increase and reaffirm their belief in such a thing, given support by their secluded community of similar believers, and supported by such practical considerations as proper diet and exercise, it is the simple fact of telling yourself, "Don't worry, we're not aging when we turn 60 or any other age. Now, let's get on with today's chores." Their minds believe, and so their bodies react and you end up with youthful looking eighty year olds.

It seems like such a simple thing to do, a simple thing to believe in, and yet how difficult it is in our world that we have to cloak such a task in ritual and ceremony in order to properly focus our minds to achieve it. It is like needing to perform a daily ritual to remind you to breath.

In short, their rituals are designed to build a "Faith Wave." A reverberating resonance of belief from one monk to another, resonating and building until it grows to the point where all within it are caught up in the firm belief of "I am young; I will achieve enlightenment and nirvana, I will free myself from suffering." If one mind can manifest change upon the world, then the collective focus of a group of them can definitely affect astounding change; like the belief-version of a laser.

So, what is the final secret of the Tibetan Monks? How do they extend youthfulness? Like everything else we have found in this book, it is belief. Mind over aging (or matter, wherein the body equals matter).

Chapter 18

HEALING AND FAITH

The term *faith healing* evokes two contrasting sets of images. The first is the tele-evangelist preacher preying on the gullible to enhance his image or line his pockets while people think themselves healed, unaware that the cancer tumor is still within them. The second image is of the unexplained, and of the possible real-life cures performed by the simple touching of a hand onto the body of another. This second image is fairly rare. The Catholic Church, for example, has verified only seventy-seven cases of genuine faith-based healing over the last two centuries, but about a thousand cases are still in question.

Yet, our interest is two-fold: (1) in the genuine, possibly miraculous healings that have their source, at least in part, in an expression of faith and (2) in the underlying physiological connection between faith and healing. We acknowledge the quacks and charlatans; you will find them in every field of endeavor. What we seek here is the deeper truth, and the science that may underlie the miraculous so that we can make the miraculous more commonplace.

Laying on of Hands

How might healing by touching or faith work? The main component is *faith* either in the one healing, in the one being healed, or both. Let us start by inserting what we know thus far.

Good
Go-
Point

The Zero Point Field surrounds us all, and indeed we are a part of it. The energy that makes up our matter is linked into the cosmic pulse of the ZPF and through that everything around us. This allows us to affect our surroundings through thought, faith, and belief. This much we have established. Another person's health is merely a part of those surroundings. Yet, as we have learned, accessing the ZPF to affect change requires a strong faith or conviction. You must be as certain of the results as you are of simple sums.

So then, even with that, why still so few bona fide healings throughout history? In the Christian Bible, Jesus heals and attributes these healings to faith of the person healed. "Your faith has made you whole." Because much of the Bible was written for simpler times to understand, let us analyze that statement with a more careful eye. What if, on a scientific level, his command to have faith to be healed is literally true?

Assume that the one doing the healing has the faith that he can affect change in someone he touches or is near; this conviction allows him to send out his energies to affect that change. But, like for any energy, we're talking about a circuit. If the one on the receiving end does not believe it can happen, then that is the same as having a firm *negative* conviction. His firm belief that nothing will happen sets up a counter flow of energy, like a wall that blocks the incoming change. The circuit remains incomplete, and thus the healing probably will not occur.

This brings up a lesson here. Your thoughts can manifest change just as everyone else's. A strong belief that change *cannot* happen is still a belief manifesting change in one's environment. In this instance, it's something that can stop others from making changes upon them. So, by *not* believing in something, you really *are* believing in something else.

Okay, so it takes faith and belief on both ends to complete a circuit, and pass along something to someone else. Got it. But, what exactly is being passed along, where is the interaction, and can we prove that it is there? Assuming that there *is* something being passed from one person to another to perform the healing, then discovering what that something is, having something like visual proof, would go a long way to increasing our belief so that we can make this sort of thing happen in our own lives. After all, it is one thing for someone to affect change within himself and heal himself from within, but causing such a change within someone else—now that is interesting.

Tibetan monks have recorded numerous examples of what people would term miraculous healings upon themselves. You have 80-year-old monks who look no older than 40 (search the Internet for a few photos on your own, if you want to see). This much is documented and agreed upon by all sides. But healing another by such things as touch is supposed to be reserved for the likes of Jesus, saints, and prophets. Or is it? Maybe he was simply trying to tell us something more.

For one person to affect another, it logically follows that there has to be something in each party with which to interact. Each one of us is connected into the ZPF and by extension into one another, but can we measure or possibly see something? We have one good candidate in the Human Energy Field.

Human Energy Field (HEF)

Our bodies are made up of particles of matter, and matter is comprised of energy. That is the light within us. We are each an organized field of molecular vibrations riding atop the quantum vibrations of the ZPF, and that light within us has its own field of subatomic vibrations. So, beneath our bodies is a structure of matter and beneath that lies a structure of quantum vibrations connected to the ZPF. But, note that we each have our own individual set of vibrations. The total of these vibrations gives us our own personal frequency.[1]

There is energy in our nervous system, energy in our thoughts, and energy in the various metabolic reactions constantly going on within us. Basic chemistry: chemical reactions give off heat and possibly light. The heat, our bodies absorb and radiate, but the light? There are

Intelesting

tiny tubules, called *tublins*, which go between the cells of our bodies, whose function is to channel this light out of our bodies. The net result of all the chemical reactions is enough to surround one with one's own energy field, and indeed it is the body's electric field that makes touch-sensitive screens possible. Now just add in the energy from the subatomic vibrations of every molecule of our bodies, and what do you get?

You get what is called the Human Energy Field, or HEF; it is known by other names such as the human aura. Yes, the faint nimbus of light that a few people can see is an actual energy field, and what's more anybody can be made to see it. In a process called Kirlian photography, invented way back in the 1930s, the aura of humans, animals, and even plants can be photographed and seen. It looks on film like an aura of light, varying in brightness in different locations of a given individual in relation to places of greater energy, sickness, or physical wounds. So there you have it, decades of photographic proof that we each have our own field of energy. It comes from within, surrounds us, and like any energy field will interact with any *other* energy field that it comes in contact with—including that of another person.

Ever feel sick or depressed around certain people? And feel more energetic and alive around others? This is part of the reason.

Our auras, or HEF if you prefer, are the net sum of every cell's vibration within us. It includes every vibratory structure and substructure, the frequency distribution of ever organ, and every bone in our bodies. This complex summation means that our individual HEFs are as unique to every one of us as fingerprints, or as our DNA. Furthermore, if a cell goes sick, the net frequencies and energy patterns of our HEF change with it; a lot of cells go sick, and the change is more perceptible. It stands to reason then, if you can affect change upon the sick parts of someone's HEF, then that change will vibrate down into the originating cells and cause them to alter in response; in effect, healing.

While this might not be the most expeditious method for, say, stitching closed an open wound before you bleed to death, it would be able to get down into cellular levels too deep for standard medical techniques currently to reach. The result of such an "aura-therapy" would seem as miraculous.

Obviously this field, our HEF, could interact with a lot more than simply the healing of others. Our auras seen and photographed are the more obvious manifestation of our connection to the ZPF. It is something that can be seen and tested, something that we can measure, and from there infer more of what we are, and what we are connected to. This HEF is what would be used by one to heal another; a healthy energy field reaching out to correct that of another, and from that act manifest a cascade of reactions within another's body that has the net result of promoting healing. And all it takes to start it off is a little faith; faith in yourself that you can perform this act, and faith by the one being healed so that he can open his own channels of energy to allow your healing energies to enter.

Okay, but then how come not everyone can see these energy fields with their naked eyes? Well, how many people have perfect 20/20 vision? How many people have better than normal hearing? Or, let's consider the belief and cultural aspect. How many people that have *never* believed in this sort of thing can see these same energy fields? None of them, for this is one of those talents where by disbelieving in it, you shut off any potential of that perception within yourself.

The Bible and similar works are big on stressing *belief* as key. This is sounding increasingly like one of those messages cloaked in the language and level of understanding of the day that it may get across one of the more subtle points of science.

Proof of the HEF

If you're suspicious of Kirlian photography, then there is something more solid on which you can lean. It has long been known that the body generates an electric field detectable at the surface of the skin, and furthermore science says that any electric field has a corresponding magnetic field in the space around it. This field was too faint to detect, so biologists and doctors long assumed it had no medical importance. But now we have the SQUID (Superconducting Quantum Interference Device), which is a magnetometer able to read the very faint magnetic fields associated with the body's various functions.

In 1963, the SQUID was first used to detect the bio-magnetic field produced by a human heart. Since then, the technique has been perfected many times over to confirm that every organ in the body has its own specific field of magnetic pulsations. In fact, now we have magneto-cardiograms and magneto-encephalograms as standard medical tools to supplement the electrocardiogram and electroencephalogram. The forefront of medical science now uses pulsating magnetic fields applied to a body's bio-magnetic field to stimulate healing of the cells and tissues to which they connect.

Why don't they use these SQUID things to measure something from one of these so-called faith healers? Well, in 1980 Dr. John Zimmerman, University of Colorado School of Medicine in Denver, did just that. He used a SQUID magnetometer to measure what might be coming from the hands of a known practitioner of touch healing. What he found was a large pulsating bio-magnetic field coming from the practitioner's hands, and sweeping a frequency range of 0.3 Hz to 30 Hz, most of the activity averaging in the 7-8 Hz range. These pulsations from the person's hands are in the same range as brain waves, and studies of frequencies necessary for healing confirm this to be the full range of therapeutic frequencies needed to stimulate healing throughout the entire body.[2]

Confirmation of these findings happened in 1992 in Japan when the study was performed on practitioners of various martial arts and Chi Gong. The energy emissions from some of them were strong enough to be detected by a simple magnetometer that was no more than a pair of coils with 80,000 turns of wire. These pulsations varied from moment to moment, and have been found to be effective for getting the healing process started even in patients that have remained unhealed for as long as 40 years. Since then, studies of such individuals have been extended to include any sound, light, and thermal fields being emitted as well.

Chakras

Chakra is the Indian name, but it is known in many other cultures by many other names. In short, if the human body has its own energy field, then a chakra is one of the focus points of this field. Like sunspots on a star, a *chakra* is a focus in our bio-magnetic field, key to the intake of energy to our bodies, and a reflection of the state of our health. Ill health means that one of the charkas wouldn't look too good, for those that can see or measure a chakra.[3]

There are said to be seven charkas, each one corresponding to a specific set of organs and endocrine gland. The seven chakras are in the Crown, the Brow, Throat, Heart, Solar Plexus, Sacral (reproductive system), and Root. Each chakra is said to absorb energy of a different frequency, directing it through internal energy meridians to those organs, which that chakra is connected. If something in one of these energy channels is damaged, either through sickness or psychological problems, then the energy will not flow properly and those that can see or detect the HEF will notice the difference. This is where some methods of "faith healing" come in. The practitioner uses his own energy to clear up the given energy channel, which then allows the body to heal itself.

Descriptions of the HEF vary from culture to culture. In India, the chakras are seen as spinning wheels while here in the West those who can see the HEF describe it as a series of vortices. The differences result from the need to describe such things in metaphor. Without the instrumentation necessary to fully record and describe what it actually appears as, metaphor must suffice as a means of those that can see, to relate it to those that cannot. While Kirlian photography can take

photos of this energy field, they are still quite crude; like the difference between old black and white television sets of the early 1950s and the plasma screens of today. We do, however, have enough mounting evidence to know that it exists, but it just remains to refine the details.

The Placebo Effect

When testing a new drug for possible medical use, to see if it is really doing anything, doctors test it against a *placebo*—an inert substance that has no active chemical or medical agent that could produce a health benefit. The person takes the placebo as if it had such an active agent. In this way, drug makers can be certain that a new drug is really doing something (or not).[4]

There is another well-known problem. For many persons, just the thought that this pill *might* cure something is enough to get their bodies and minds back to doing their job. Even more unusual, it seems that the effects of placebo-induced curing have been getting stronger when compared to medical trials done in 1980. This has prompted researchers to delve more into the biology behind the placebo effect itself.

Placebos started as an outright lie back in World War II when an Army nurse was assisting anesthetist Henry Beecher and morphine supplies had run low. The nurse told a wounded patient that the shot she was giving him was a powerful painkiller, even though it was just salt water. The shot still relieved the soldier's agony and forestalled the onset of shock. Since then, researchers have found that placebo responses stem from active processes in the brain.

The faith or belief that a patient has in a medical cure starts the brain to altering the body's metabolic processes in response, releasing hormones and immune responses to affect a physical cure, or at least start things on their way. This shows what we have been asserting, that *belief* in something is key. Faith healing is all a matter of belief, as is healing by meditation, and any other activity that involves the mind. Your thoughts affect change upon yourself and the world around you, in this specific case inducing cures within your very own body. This is not some vague esoteric philosophy, not some magic spell, nothing involving kneeling before an idol—unless you really want to. It is an effect rooted in medical science, backed by decades of data, and known the world over and accepted by solid science. Healing by way of placebo is fact.

So, what then is the big mystery behind faith healing or any other touch or remote healing, for that matter? At the risk of being flippant, faith healing is the placebo effect at a distance.

Chapter 19

ALTERED STATES
OF
CONSCIOUSNESS

Out of body experiences, going astral, hypnosis, and other altered states of consciousness are often viewed with caution and suspicion. Some have used drugs or special mushrooms to achieve an altered state, the benefits being questionable and the results quite often dangerous to one's health. The question then arises, are the persons really in an altered state or merely hallucinating? Part of the problem, I would think, is a lack of a good definition of what exactly an altered state is. To know that, we also need a good definition of consciousness.[1]

We have talked about brain waves, the different types, and their probable functions. We know now that consciousness may lie somewhere deep in the Gamma part of the brain's E-M spectrum and that our minds are governed by the same equations as the rest of quantum mechanics, but is there more to it? Is there more that will help us to understand it and help explain altered states of consciousness and observed psychic phenomena?

The *Out of Body Experience*, or OBE, occurs when someone perceives their consciousness as leaving their body, observing their body from the outside, and traveling away for a time. In times past, this was also known as astral projection. In either case, the mind is said to transcend great distances in a very short time; so short a time, in fact, that one would have to invoke the speed of light and relativistic effects for it to work. To achieve an OBE, the subject has to first bring himself to a near unconscious state. His body is completely inactive, the mind is completely focused. The mind has generated its Faith Wave state.

The Near Death Experience, or NDE, is another related form of an altered state. Here, the subject is unconscious and near death. He then leaves his body. At first, he sees that which is surrounding it, and then travels off into another realm or reality, and into a place of bright lights and often a tunnel of light. After lingering for a bit, the subject then returns to his body as he is brought back from the brink of death.

These two examples both look extremely similar and probably invoke the same mechanism. In both cases, the subject is unconscious, and the mind freed for a time of direct connection with the body whether it be from being extremely focused through some form of meditation, or focused by the leering face of Death. We know that the body has its own energy field and that the mind is a collection of self-aware standing waves, so the ability to leave the body as a separate E-M field is within the realm of possibility. But, traveling to distant places? Traveling through a tunnel of light? How do we explain these?

Dreaming is another altered state of consciousness. Think about it. When you dream, you are completely unaware of the outside world, and your perceptions are turned completely inward. You are completely focused only on what is inside of your own mind. Your thoughts become your reality and can often act to help you sort things out or help you solve problems that you've had at the back of your mind. You are able to concentrate in a way that you never could while awake.

So, an altered state involves achieving some kind of mental focus. This sounds exactly like what meditation is supposed to do. A centering of one's self with the goal of complete mental focus and a way of concentrating, on concentration itself, until a miraculous state of mind is achieved. Meditation, then, can be an altered state.

So is hypnosis. Many people view hypnosis as the subject being in a sort of sleep-like trance, but research is showing this is not to be the case. The subject is fully aware and awake; they are merely focusing their attention inward with little awareness of what lies outside their bodies, save the hypnotist voicing the suggestions. Try focusing your attention on just one thing to the exclusion of all else. It becomes your entire world. You could have someone talking to you and be completely oblivious to their presence. You know only that which you are trying to do, and will devote your complete resources to finishing that perfectly.

A person under hypnosis is in a state of hyper-attention and is fixated on the one object the hypnotist used to fix his attention on. He is never asleep, never under someone's control, just fixated on one thing to the exclusion of all else. In short, he has achieved an altered state of consciousness through the help of another. While in this state, one can accurately recall past memories, relive previous experiences, heighten some senses, block the feeling of pain, and even hear and feel things that are not there, based upon suggestions from the hypnotist.

In deeper hypnosis, it has even been confirmed that the body is better able to heal from disease and injury. This is precisely like the case for meditation. People in a deep meditative trance have displayed miracles of self-healing. How can this occur? Consider that in such a state, your mind is now devoted entirely to but one thing. It does not matter if this is healing or solving a specific problem. If the entire resources of your mind and body are completely devoted to just a single task, then it is going to be performing that task a whole lot more efficiently. Just like while sleeping, your mind is in the Delta state where your body performs most of its healing, as you sleep.

Researchers have confirmed that there are specific patterns of brain waves associated with someone under hypnosis. This shows that hypnosis is a solid observable effect. Some researchers have even divided hypnosis into six different levels.

— The first level allows the subject to open his eyes while still under suggestion.

— The second level allows for arm and hand muscle control through suggestion.

— Level three is aphasia, where through suggestion the subject is able to block a number or word from his memory.

— The fourth level allows enhanced recall of past events, and light anesthesia can be reached.

— The fifth allows subjects to re-live previous experiences as well as having heightened visual, auditory, and kinesthetic senses.

— Finally, the sixth level is the deepest state, where through suggestion a subject can be told to see, feel, hear, and smell something that is not there.

It's starting to sound like our Faith Wave is yet another altered state. Or perhaps it's the other way around—that hypnosis, OBEs, and the rest are simply manifestations of the mind in its Faith Wave state. We have earlier postulated that Faith Wave is generated by the Gamma and other waveforms common to focused, nearly unconscious states, but this is exactly the state the brain is in while engaged in OBEs, NDEs, hypnosis, and other altered states. One proves the other. Call it an altered state, Faith Wave, or being one with the Universe, but such states involve the mind generating a very specific range of frequencies and waveforms, ones that are measurable by scientific instrumentation, and as real as sunlight, apples, or your pulse.

So, while such altered states are proved to be possible, how can such states be achieved? What is the science and reason behind them? The answer may lie in the nature of what we are and how we think. Science has piece together how a person, or even an animal, can think and react so quickly when the physical processes behind it are so slow. Brain cells are chemical in nature, as are the signals speeding through them.

But at the speeds they are limited to, we would be operating several times slower than we actually do. Synapses directly contacting one another are fine for certain types of communication and access, but not for the whole picture.

The solution was first suggested in a 1997 paper by Yugoslavian researchers. In that paper, it was pointed out that brain waves are, in fact, actual waves. Like a wave front sweeping across the ocean, the net result of the dense collection of neurons is a collective field that sweeps through the mind as a whole. So weak of a field that researchers long assumed it was not strong enough to allow cross-chatter beyond the range of a synapse's gap. But in this paper, it is pointed out, and accompanied by an extensive variety of complex mathematics, that brain waves of Ultra Low Frequency (ULF) can traverse the brain as a whole, triggering synaptic activity in parallel cells, and at much higher speeds.[2]

Two things happen as a result of this explanation. As you might expect, the brain behaves as a quantum computer. That often sought after golden ring that computer scientists are now trying to reach, if it were designed and built, would create a computer with more computing power than the rest of the world put together... which is sort of what the capacity of one human brain is right now anyway.

Further supporting this idea is the presence of those tublins previously mentioned. Neurons are composed of a skeleton of microtubules, each constructed from tublins, and a type of hexagonal shaped protein. Within these microstructures, researcher Stuart Hameroff has discovered a generation of highly coherent laser-like light, which could act as the quantum bit, or *qbit*, of a quantum computer. These bio-photons have been observed by others, emerging outside the bodies of not just humans but other life forms as well, and may be related back to the DNA. At any rate, where you have photons, you have quantum entanglement, and in this case the enormous potential of a natural biological quantum computer.

What?

The other consequence comes from the fact that such a wave is now purely Electro-Magnetic and not limited to the speed of the much slower chemical reactions going from synapse to synapse directly. This fact invokes the possibility of relativistic speeds. I will state that again; the ionic medium of the brain generates an EM field of relativistic velocities while also operating as a quantum computer.

At this point, the math gets even hairier. This single supposition makes possible such altered states. Once relativity is involved, you open the possibility of such long range interactions as described by certain psychic phenomena, including a biologically generated spatio-temporal tunneling, much like an Einstein-Rosen space-time bridge, or wormhole. This makes such things as astral projection, OBEs, and NDEs quite possible.

Spiritual healing, or healing by touch, can now be explained by an exchange of ions and E-M fields with another in close proximity, which is an exchange that the world fills in what that other person's body needs to repair itself.

Go back to the quantum computing for a bit. Recall the property of quantum particles that they are neither a wave nor a particle until they are measured. Our brains are comprised of those very same particles. When we are awake, we take in sensory input, we are fully aware of our surroundings, constantly processing information, and in short fully aware of our self. The electrons in our brains behave like particles, so we are completely unaware of the rest of the cosmos out there. But asleep, when we lose this self-image for a while and have no sensory input, our electrons behave like waves, allowing our consciousness to touch upon its entanglement with the rest of the universe and travel as a nonmaterial entity. We wake up, and our wave function collapses back into being particle-like.

Cutting-edge researchers are now confirming the definition of consciousness as a nonmaterial entity capable of independent external existence similar to the electron in the famous double slit experiment.

Like that electron, it cannot only change itself, but whatever it comes in contact with, which is to say the reality around it. But, unlike the electron, consciousness is self-aware, and can control itself as it desires without waiting for external influences.

In sum, consciousness can change reality just by being aware that it can do so.

If you want to change what you are looking at; change the way you are looking.

Chapter 20

CONCLUSIONS

We are a part of God and the ZPF. When we pray, meditate, or focus to manifest a change in our reality, we are trying to access God's power, trying to access the Zero Point Field. Call God by whichever name you want, or call the Divine by no name at all. Call God science or religion or the Force, but there is no denying the presence. The Universe is alive, intelligent, and asking of our needs, for it is us and just waiting to hear what we need.

So, it would seem that religion has had some science within it after all. Such concepts as quantum entanglement, the Zero Point Field, particle-wave duality, and even the simple photon—these would have been well beyond the minds of persons four or five thousand years ago. It was easier to just tell the people that it's all God and God's power. Trying to explain a Universe that is both intelligent and encompassing of all intelligences, would be like giving a definition of what God is anyway. The concept of how our thoughts can manifest in our reality, direct it, provide the act of creation itself? Nothing anyone back then would have been able to fathom, so best to just tell them, "Pray to God who will grant your desire."

Should this lessen what God is in anyone's eyes? No. Worship God whichever way you want, in whichever name you want, or don't call God a god at all, but simply a universal quantum field to be accessed by a focused mindset that resembles prayer. It doesn't matter. What matters is the end result. History has provided us with examples of miracles that have manifested as a result of focused thoughts in the form of prayers. In the Far East there are examples of monks deep in meditation who can perform seeming miracles upon their own bodies. God or the Zero Point Field is there waiting to be directed and waiting to fulfill one's needs. Whether through prayer, meditation, or manifesting, this is all the same thing. Our thoughts can direct matter, stir events, and manifest what we seek and need.

So what is God? What is the Zero Pont Field? The same answer can be used for both, and that is that God or ZPF is collectively every one of us and in every thing in Creation. We are God, along with the whole of Creation. The sacred texts of Christians, for example, offer many teachings that agree:

— "For from him, and through him and to him are all things" *(Romans 8.36 NIV).*
— "In him we live, and move, and have our being. We are his offspring" *(Acts 17.28 NIV).*
— "There is one God who is father of all, over all, through all and within all." *(Letter to the Ephesians 4.6).*

When humanity as a whole feels a need, the ZPF (or God) manifests a possible solution; a prophet or influential teacher, or even Savior, perhaps. When you as an individual feel a need, pray for it, meditate on it, or otherwise focus your thoughts on it. Then a possible solution will manifest itself. It won't knock you on the head. You will need to be on the lookout for this manifested solution or divine intervention. The Universe will give you what you ask for, but not always post a spotlight directly at what's been waiting for you to find.

Miracles of faith or meditation, psychic abilities, magic—all of it is simply the result of someone interacting with the infinite potential of the ZPF, with God. Faith in yourself or a supreme deity is the key to achieving the focus necessary to manifest these miraculous happenings. Just remember that you are always manifesting, always praying, and even if you do not realize it. The difference is in taking conscious control over what you are praying *for.*

Pray for it, believe in it, and it will come. Be ready to adjust your behaviors and thoughts accordingly. Then, be alert for the signs manifesting what you seek. The solution has been around since ancient times, but we were too young as a species to comprehend it. We are no longer children now, and we are ready to listen and understand the more technical details of the message. Perhaps, knowing this will help us get a clearer connection with the ZPF, or universal deity. Belief is all important to manifesting our thoughts into our reality. You can manifest your deepest needs and desires. Quiet your mind, intend, declare, and then detach, knowing you will achieve what you are seeking. Add a foundation of faith, align your behaviors, words, and thoughts, and then allow the Universe to go to work for you. You now have the recipe for the secret to manifesting your desires; in fact, you have had it all along—*Faith Wave.*

I think therefore it is.

NOTES

Introduction

1. For information about Zero Point Field, see http://en.wikipedia. org/wiki/Zero-point_energy. Bernard Haisch, *The God Theory: Universes, Zero-Point Field, and What's Behind It All* (Weiser Books, 2009). Lynne McTaggert, *The Field: The Quest for the Secret Force of the Universe* (Harper Perennial, 2008).

2. For a detailed report of my living with Tibetan monks, see *Think Yourself Young* (Intelegance, 2011), chapter 21.

3. See, *The Point of Power* (Intelegance, 2010), Part 1.

4. Allan Williams, *Brainwave Basics – Stuff You Should Know in Words You Can Understand About Using Brain Waves to Train Your Brain* (PowerMeUp Publishing, 2012).

5. See, for example, "Buddha on the Brain" (http://www.wired. com/wired/archive/14.02/dalai.html) and "Links between Dalai Lama and Neuroscience" (http://www.npr.org/templates/story/ story.php?storyId=5008565).

6. See *Point of Power*, chapter 13.

Chapter 1:
Quantum Mechanics Basics

1. See *Point of Power,* chapters 7-8.

2. J.L. Heilbron, *Dilemmas of an Upright Man: Max Planck and the Fortunes of German Science* (Harvard University Press, 2000).

3. Albert Einstein, *Ideas and Opinions* (Broadway, 1995).

4. See, for example, "Particle-wave duality" (http://hyperphysics. phy-astr.gsu.edu/hbase/mod1.html).

5. See, for example, "Particle-wave duality" (http://hyperphysics. phy-astr.gsu.edu/hbase/mod1.html).

6. See, for example, "Copenhagen Interpretation" (http:// en.wikipedia.org/wiki/Copenhagen_Interpretation).

7. For information about Schrödinger's equation, see *hyperphysics. phy-astr.gsu.edu/hbase/quantum/schr.html*

Chapter 2:
The Uncertainty Principle and Entanglement

1. Steven Holzner, *Quantum Physics* (For Dummies Publisher, 2009). For an online cheat sheet, see (http://www.dummies. com/how-to/content/quantum-physics-and-the-heisenberg-uncertainty-pri.html).

2. Albert Einstein, *Ideas and Opinions* (Broadway, 1995).

3. Brian Clegg, *The God Effect: Quantum Entanglement, Science's Strangest Phenomenon* (St. Martin's Griffin, 2009), 32-51.

4. For information about Zero Point Field, see http://en.wikipedia. org/wiki/Zero-point_energy. Bernard Haisch, *The God Theory: Universes, Zero-Point Field, and What's Behind It All* (Weiser

Books, 2009). Lynne McTaggert, *The Field: The Quest for the Secret Force of the Universe* (Harper Perennial, 2008).

Chapter 3:
The Mind and Quantum Mechanics

1. See *Point of Power*, chaps. 9-11.

2. See *Point of Power*, Introduction and chaps. 12-13.

3. James Simmonds, *A First Look at Perturbation Theory* (Dover Books, 1997).

4. *Point of Power*, chap. 9.

5. *Point of Power*, chap. 10. Andrew Newberg et al., *Why God Won't Go Away: Brain Science and the Biology of Belief* (Ballentine Books, 2002). David R. Hawkins, *Healing and Recovery* (Veritas Publishing, 2009); see also, David R. Hawkins, *Transcending the Levels of Consciousness: The Stairway to Enlightenment* (Veritas Publishing, 2006).

Chapter 4:
Brain Waves

1. Allan Williams, *Brainwave Basics - Stuff You Should Know in Words You Can Understand About Using Brain Waves to Train Your Brain* (PowerMeUp Publishing, 2012).

2. Andrew Newberg et al., *Why God Won't Go Away: Brain Science and the Biology of Belief* (Ballentine Books, 2002).

3. Ilchi Lee, *Brain Wave Vibration: Getting Back into the Rhythm of a Happy, Healthy Life*, 2nd ed. (Best Life Media, 2010).

Chapter 5:
Neuroplasticity

1. Jeffrey Schwartz, *The Mind and the Brain: Neuroplasticity and the Power of Mental Force* (Harper Perennial, 2003).

2. Daniel Siegel, *Mindsight: The New Science of Personal Transformation* (Bantam, 2010).

3. See Michael Merzenich's website (http://merzenich.positscience.com/?page_id=143)

4. For the FastForWord product, see (http://www.scilearn.com/products/)

5. "Dalai Lama and Neuroscience" National Public Radio (http://www.npr.org/templates/story/story.php?storyId=5008565); "Dalai Lama Donates to University of Wisconsin" New York Times (http://www.nytimes.com/2010/09/27/us/27happy.html); Dalai Lama dialogues with Richard Davidson (*www.wildmind.org/tag/richard-davidson)*

6. http://www.skewsme.com/implants.html#axzz1pQX6LWQD

Chapter 6:
The Zero Point Field

1. See, for example (http://en.wikipedia.org/wiki/Vacuum_state)

2. See (http://en.wikipedia.org/wiki/Casmir_Effect)

3. Peter Galison, *How Experiments End* (Univ. of Chicago Press, 1987)

4. Margaret Cheney, *Tesla: Man Out of Time* (Touchstone, 2001)

5. For details, see (http://prb.aps.org/abstract/PRB/v26/i1/p74_1)

6. Fritz-Albert Popp, et al., editors, *What Is Life? Scientific Approaches and Philosophical Positions* (World Scientific, 2002)

7. Lynne McTaggert, *The Field: The Quest for the Secret Force of the Universe* (Harper Perennial, 2008)

8. Doug Bennett, *Life and Spirit in the Quantum Field: Spirit Is Real, Feelings Rule, and Other Adventures in the Quantum Life* (Take Charge Books, 2010)

Chapter 7:
The ZPF and Mass

1. Bernard Haisch, Alfonso Rueda, and H. E. Puthoff, "Beyond E=MC^2," *The Sciences* (Dec. 1994): (http://www.calphysics.org/haisch/sciences.html)

2. Lynne McTaggert, *The Field: The Quest for the Secret Force of the Universe* (Harper Perennial, 2008)

3. http://en.wikipedia.org/wiki/Andrei_Sakharov

Chapter 8:
Religions of Abraham

1. (http://en.wikipedia.org/wiki/Religion)

2. George Robinson, *Essential Judaism: A Complete Guide to Beliefs, Customs, and Rituals* (Atria Books, 2001), and Wayne Dosick, *Living Judaism: The Complete Guide to Jewish Belief, Tradition, and Practice* (Harper One, 1998).

3. Alister McGrath, *Christianity: An Introduction* (Blackwell, 2006), and Linda Woodhead, *Christianity: A Very Short Introduction* (Oxford, 2005).

4. Annemarie Schimmel, *Islam: An Introduction* (SUNY Press, 1992), and Shaykh Fadhlalla Haeri, *The Essential Message of the Qur'an* (Winchester, U.K., 2011).

Chapter 9:
Religions of Insight

1. Kim Knott, *Hinduism: A Very Short Introduction* (Oxford, 2000), and Gavin Flood, *An Introduction to Hinduism* (Cambridge, 1996). For an overview, see also (http://en.wikipedia.org/wiki/Religion)

2. Damien Keown, *Buddhism: A Very Short Introduction* (Oxford, 2000), and Huston Smith, *Buddhism: A Concise Introduction* (Harper One, 2004).

3. C. Scott Littleton, *Shinto: Origins, Rituals, Festivals, Spirits, Sacred Places* (Oxford, 2002), and Sokyo Ono, *Shinto the Kami Way* (Tuttle, 1994).

4. Jacob Neusner and Bruce Chilton, *The Golden Rule: The Ethics of Reciprocity in World Religions* (Continuum, 2009), and Lawrence Becker, *Reciprocity* (Univ. of Chicago Press, 1990).

Chapter 10:
Miracles

1. Richard Bartlett, *The Physics of Miracles: Tapping into the Field of Consciousness Potential* (Atria, 2010).

2. Arthur Waskow and Phyllis Berman, *Freedom Journeys: The Tale of Exodus and Wilderness across the Millennia* (Jewish Lights, 2011).

3. http://en.wikipedia.org/wiki/Our_Lady_of_the_Cape#The_ Miracle_of_the_Ice_Bridge

4. Chauncay Crandall, *Raising the Dead: A Doctor Encounters the Miraculous* (FaithWords, 2010).

5. Angelo Pastrovicchi, *St. Joseph of Copetino* (Tan, 2009).

6. Pamela Rae Heath, *Mind–Matter Interaction: A Review of Historical Reports, Theory, and Research* (McFarland, 2011).

7. Jacalyn Duffin, *Medical Miracles: Doctors, Saints, and Healing in the Modern World* (Oxford, 2008).

Chapter 11:
Meditation, Prayer, and Faith

1. Mihaly Csikszentmihalyi, *Flow: The Psychology of Optimal Experience* (Univ. of Chicato, 2008); see also, *Point of Power*, chap. 11.

2. http://austega.com/gifted/16-gifted/articles/24-flow-and-mihaly-csikszentmihalyi.html

Chapter 12:
Meditating on Miracles

1. See, for example, Thich Nhat Hanh et al., *The Miracle of Mindfulness: An Introduction to the Practice of Meditation* (Beacon, 1999).

2. Kimberly Schneider, *Everything You Need Is Right Here: Five Steps to Manifesting Magic and Miracles* (Avalon Emerging Press, 2012).

3. See *Point of Power*, chap. 14.

4. Jesus, for example, began his ministry by fasting and wandering in the wilderness for 40 days.

5. *Point of Power*, chap. 12.

Chapter 13:
Magic

1. Two excellent books on this subject are Kimberly Schneider, *Everything You Need Is Right Here: Five Steps to Manifesting Magic and Miracles* (Avalon Emerging Press, 2012); and Kenneth Woodward, *The Book of Miracles: The Meaning of Miracle Stories in Christianity, Judaism, Buddhism, Hinduism, and Islam* (Simon and Schuster, 2001).

2. Eliot Pattison, *The Skull Mantra* (St. Martin Press, 2001).

3. Randall Styers, *Making Magic: Religion, Magic, and Science in the Modern World* (Oxford Univ. Press, 2004).

4. Raymond Buckland, *Witchcraft from the Inside: Origins of the Fastest Growing Religious Movement in America* (Llewellyn, 1995).

Chapter 14:
Science versus Religion

1. Elaine Howard Ecklund, *Science vs. Religion: What Scientists Really Think* (Oxford Univ. Press, 2004).

2. *Point of Power*, chap. 9.

3. Bernard Haisch, *The God Theory: The Universes, Zero Point Fields, and What's behind It All* (Weiser Books, 2009).

Chapter 15:
What Is God?

1. Andrew Newberg et al., *Why God Won't Go Away: Brain Science and the Biology of Belief* (Ballentine Books, 2002).

Shinto: C. Scott Littleton, *Shinto: Origins, Rituals, Festivals, Spirits, Sacred Places* (Oxford, 2002), and Sokyo Ono, *Shinto the Kami Way* (Tuttle, 1994).

Buddhism: Damien Keown, *Buddhism: A Very Short Introduction* (Oxford, 2000), and Huston Smith, *Buddhism: A Concise Introduction* (Harper One, 2004).

Hinduism: Kim Knott, *Hinduism: A Very Short Introduction* (Oxford, 2000), and Gavin Flood, *An Introduction to Hinduism* (Cambridge, 1996).

Judaism: George Robinson, *Essential Judaism: A Complete Guide to Beliefs, Customs, and Rituals* (Atria Books, 2001), and Wayne Dosick, *Living Judaism: The Complete Guide to Jewish Belief, Tradition, and Practice* (Harper One, 1998).

Christianity: Alister McGrath, *Christianity: An Introduction* (Blackwell, 2006), and Linda Woodhead, *Christianity: A Very Short Introduction* (Oxford, 2005).

Islam: Annemarie Schimmel, *Islam: An Introduction* (SUNY Press, 1992), and Shaykh Fadhlalla Haeri, *The Essential Message of the Qur'an* (Winchester, U.K., 2011).

2. *Point of Power*, chap. 10 and Part 3.

Chapter 16:
Belief versus Imagining

1. *Point of Power,* chaps. 9, 12, and 14.

Chapter 17:
Tibetan Monks

1. See, Peter Baksa, *Think Yourself Young* (Intelegance, 2011), chap. 21.

Chapter 18:
Healing and Faith

1. Colin Ross, *Human Energy Fields: A New Science and Medicine* (Manitou Communications, 2009).

2. There are a number of accounts of this, for example, (http://www.pemft.net/part-2-frequency.html).

3. See, Liz Simpson, *Book of Chakras Healing* (SOS Free Stock, 2005); and, Cindi Dale, *The Complete Book of Chakra Healing: Activate the Transformative Power of Your Energy Centers* (Llewellyn, 2009).

4. Fabrizio Benedetti, *Placebo Effects: Understanding the Mechanisms in Health and Disease* (Oxford Univ. Press, 2008).

Chapter 19:
Altered States of Consciousness

1. See, Charles Tart, *States of Consciousness* (iUniverse, 2001); Ronald Havens, *Self-Hypnosis for Cosmic Consciousness: Achieving*

Altered States, Mystical Experiences and Spiritual Enlightenment (Crown House, 2007); and Deane H. Shapiro, *Meditation: Self-Regulation Strategy and Altered State of Consciousness* (Aldine Transaction, 2008).

2. Jean L. Rasson and Todor Delipetrov, eds., *Geomagnetics for Aeronautical Safety: A Case Study in and around the Balkans* (Nato Security through Science Series, 2006).